THE DARWEN COUNTY HISTORY SERIES

A History of
SUFFOLK

Packhorse bridge of the 15th century, Moulton.

A History of
SUFFOLK

David Dymond
and Peter Northeast

Drawings by
**Joanna Northeast,
Eleanor and Catherine Dymond**

Phillimore

1995

Published by
PHILLIMORE & CO. LTD.
Shopwyke Manor Barn, Chichester, West Sussex

First published 1985
Revised edition 1995

© David Dymond and Peter Northeast, 1985, 1995

ISBN 0 85033 938 3

Printed and bound in Great Britain by
BUTLER & TANNER LTD.
Frome, Somerset

Contents

TO OUR PARENTS

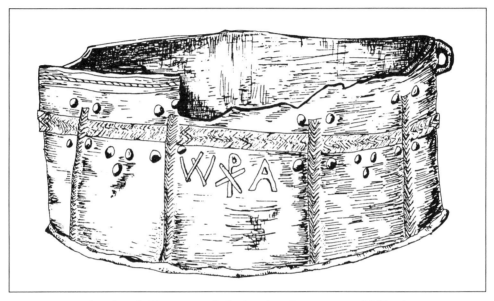

Lead tank with Christian symbols, found at Roman town of Icklingham.

List of Illustrations

Frontispiece: Packhorse bridge of the 15th century, Moulton

List of Colour Plates

Acknowledgements

In the preparation of this book, we have received invaluable help and encouragement from many friends and colleagues. We would like to thank the staffs of the Suffolk Record Office, Cambridge University Library and Suffolk Archaeological Unit, and the following individuals: John Blatchly, David Butcher, Tony Copsey, Timothy Easton, Frank Grace, Edward Martin, Pat Murrell, Clive Paine, Judith Plouviez, Margaret Statham, Gwyn Thomas, Stanley West and the late Pat Woodgate. Our special thanks are due to Elsie McCutcheon for criticising our sometimes tortured prose; Nancy Tripp for typing several drafts; our daughters, Joanna Northeast, Eleanor Dymond and Catherine Dymond, for drawing the marginal illustrations; and Geoff Cordy who uncomplainingly took or processed most of the photographs.

For supplying individual plates and maps, and for granting us permission to reproduce them, we wish to acknowledge the following persons and institutions: The British Library, Department of Manuscripts, VI; Cambridge University Collection of Air Photographs, 10, 24, 49; Cambridge University Library, 71; Geoff Cordy, 32-4, 37, 48, 58, 61, 95, 117, 120, 122, 156; the late Richard Deeks, 145; Timothy Easton, 86; T.M. Felgate, 90; Felixstowe Dock and Railway Company, 142; Sue and Mike Finch, 68; M.J. Hardy, 18; Judith Plouviez, 16; University of Reading, Institute of Agricultural History and Museum of English Rural Life, 111, 126; Suffolk Record Office, 105, 127, 131, 143; Keith Wade, 27 and David Wordley, 56. We also acknowledge the help of John Blatchly, who kindly lent us the materials to make 13, 65, 99, 124 and 135.

Preface

It is a privilege to be asked to write the history of an English county, and a double privilege if one is not a native. Neither of us was born in Suffolk, but as newcomers we fell under its subtle spell, and have studied and taught its history for more than 20 years. In this book we have been given the task of distilling 400,000 years of local life into 130 pages. Naturally there are many omissions, and some readers will look in vain for their own favourite topics, characters and places. Nevertheless, we have deliberately tried to paint a broad picture, and to summarise what we see as the most important trends in county life. This, we hope, will help to make sense of what happened in individual villages and towns, and also provide strong links with history at a national level. We have particularly tried to incorporate the new approaches and recent work which, in the last generation, have transformed our view of Suffolk's past.

The state of Local History is said to be more flourishing in Suffolk than anywhere else in England. Certainly, more searchers visit the Suffolk Record Office than any other, and publications pour unceasingly from the press. Meanwhile, a growing army of individuals, amateur and professional, is beavering away, and new research groups and societies spring up every year. A particularly encouraging sign is that schoolchildren and students are flocking to the Record Office, and acquiring the skills of historical enquiry at a much earlier age than used to be the case. If this book helps to stimulate more research which will modify or challenge what we have written, then we shall feel more than rewarded. We believe that Local History is more than an absorbing interest and more, indeed, than an academic subject; it brings people together to discuss and discover the complicated truth of human affairs, and helps us to appreciate the character and evolution of the communities in which we live. The quest to understand our local and regional heritage has only just begun, and the opportunities for new work are both exciting and endless.

DAVID DYMOND
PETER NORTHEAST

1

Prehistory and the Romans

The first inhabitants of the area we now call Suffolk were hunters and food-gatherers who arrived during a warm phase of the Ice Age, probably around 400,000 B.C. This was the beginning of the Old Stone Age or Palaeolithic which was about 40 times longer than the rest of human history. As the Ice Age contained many warmer phases, each 20-30,000 years long, hunting parties must have entered and left the region many times. Whenever the climate improved, the glaciers melted back to the north and vegetation slowly reclothed the landscape, beginning with sparse tundra and culminating in mature forest; meanwhile, small groups of hunters, warily following the tracks of animals, established their own seasonal camps and routes. They retreated southwards only when the ice-sheets again threatened to engulf the living environment. Man-made clearings, rough shelters and tracks were obliterated by later waves of ice yet, paradoxically, stone implements of the Old Stone Age are frequently found embedded in glacial clays, sands and gravels. So great is the quantity that East Anglia has been called 'the meeting ground of geology and prehistoric archaeology'. This reflects not the size of Palaeolithic population, which at any phase probably consisted of no more than a few family groups, but their frequent making and discarding of tools over an immensely long period of time.

1 *Hand-axe of Acheulian type, over nine inches long, found at Hoxne.*

At High Lodge, Mildenhall, which has been described as 'among the oldest and best preserved archaeological sites in Europe', flake-tools discovered in the 1960s are the earliest known man-made artefacts in Suffolk, more than 400,000 years old. On the other side of the county, the Gipping valley has produced a wide range of Palaeolithic implements which imply intermittent occupation over several hundreds of thousands of years. The most important site of the period is, however, at Hoxne. Here, in an old brickpit, a discovery was made in 1797 which is not only important in itself but 'marks the beginning of scientific archaeology'. A local antiquary called John Frere found chipped flint hand-axes in a gravelly soil 12 feet below the surface. Although he assumed that they were 'weapons of war' rather than all-purpose tools he reasoned brilliantly that they were 'fabricated and used by a people who had not the use of metals' and referred them 'to a very remote period indeed; even beyond that of the present world'.

The most recent excavation at Hoxne was directed by John Wymer in the 1970s. In the sediments that gradually filled a prehistoric lake, he found two stratified groups of 'Acheulian' hand-axes and flakes where they had been used and dropped by hunter-gatherers 350,000-300,000 years ago. The implements

2 *The Orwell Estuary looking towards the sea: one of the major gateways into Suffolk from prehistoric to modern times.*

3 *Bronze socketed axe, with loop for binding it to wooden handle, found at Lakenheath.*

had been used for various purposes: to cut meat, chop and bore bones, cut plants, scrape and cut hides, and to work wood. In climates generally colder and wetter than our own, parties of hunters had stalked a range of animals: their main diet was horse and deer but they also fed on lemming, bison, rhinoceros and elephant.

When the glaciers finally retreated around 10,000 B.C., plants and animals recolonised the landscape for the last time. As in the warmer phases of the Ice Age, tundra gave way to birch woods which in turn were succeeded by true forest. Today in places like Staverton Thicks and the Bradfield Woods there are probably fragments of the 'wildwood' which regenerated in post-glacial times, and which has been modified by centuries of human management. To cope with this forested environment, human groups developed a new Mesolithic technology which included hafted axes and composite weapons for hunting, fishing and fowling. Many of their characteristic 'microliths' have been found in Suffolk, usually, unfortunately on the surface rather than stratified. For their seasonal habitations they favoured two kinds of places. They liked well-drained sandy soils where the natural woodland was not too dense as at Wangford and Lakenheath where several productive sites have been known since the early 1960s. Alternatively they chose to live beside streams, lakes and marshes where they lived off abundant animals, birds, fish and plants. For example, the small island beside the river Lark at West Stow, later occupied by the Anglo-Saxon village, had been inhabited about 5,000 years earlier by Mesolithic hunters.

By cutting down trees and using fire, Mesolithic groups must have punched many holes in the natural forest but the extent of such clearances is not known nor is it known whether the trees always reclaimed the ground they had lost. At the very least, human activities were probably altering the composition of the 'wildwood' by encouraging vigorous species like hazel and discouraging poor polinators like lime.

During the long Ice Age and for thousands of years after, sea level was much lower than it is today. The southern end of what is now the North Sea was exposed land, much of it marshy. Eastward-flowing rivers of East Anglia, like the Stour and Waveney, were then tributaries of the Thames and Rhine. As the glaciers and ice-sheets continued to melt, sea level rose, the North Sea grew southwards, and East Anglia began to take on its familiar rounded shape. Around 7000 B.C., the last narrow bridge of land connecting eastern England to the continent was severed and our history as an island began.

4 *Collared and decorated urn of the Bronze Age, found at Snape.*

In the Neolithic period, which began soon after 5000 B.C., man's control of the environment improved dramatically. For example, he possessed efficient axes of flint and other stone, often ground and polished, and had developed the technique of coppicing. This involved the cutting of trees and shrubs to the ground, to encourage the growth of multiple straight poles which could be regularly harvested at varying sizes. The flint-mines of Grimes Graves were in full production from about 2600 B.C., and sending high-quality flint along the Icknield Way to many other parts of Britain. At the same time, traders were bringing implements of other kinds of stone into East Anglia, by land and water, from relatively distant places such as Cornwall, Wales and the Lake District. Neolithic axes have been found in many parts of Suffolk, particularly in the south-east near Ipswich and on the Breckland. Even the centre of the county, where the boulder clay was most heavily forested, has yielded a thin scatter of axes. Palaeobotanists now argue that clearance was under way in Suffolk by 3700 B.C., and was especially effective on lighter soils. On the Breckland, for example, Neolithic settlers removed most of the natural woodland and trees were not seen again, in large numbers at least, until the 19th century.

The Neolithic inhabitants of Suffolk were its first farmers; they were clearing land because they had learned to domesticate animals and grow crops. They continued to hunt and gather food from the wild, but this merely supplemented a new and fundamentally different way of life. Farming, by giving a more assured supply of food, encouraged the growth of population, the building of more permanent settlements, greater social and economic differentiation, and more specialisation.

Some of these trends are illustrated at Hurst Fen, Mildenhall, where the debris of a Neolithic farmstead of about 3500 B.C. covered an area of 180 by 90 yards. The site yielded numerous small hollows which were interpreted as storage-pits, though some could have been post-holes from buildings. The inhabitants had worked flint expertly as witnessed by their delicate leaf-shaped arrowheads. They also had quantities of pottery, a newly invented material which facilitated the storage, preparation and cooking of food and drink. The pots had rounded bases and some were decorated with lines and impressions.

5 *Neolithic flint axe, found at Mildenhall Fen.*

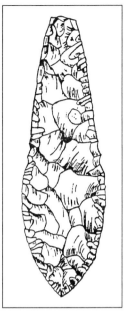

6 *Knife of knapped flint, early Bronze Age, found at Lakenheath.*

Most crucial of all, evidence was found that this was truly a farming community: saddle-querns and rubbers had been used to grind cereals, while fragments of pottery were found to contain the impressions of emmer-wheat and barley.

The growing complexity of Neolithic society is best illustrated by an ability to organise major projects for communal purposes. Suffolk already has three examples of 'causewayed camps'. These are large enclosures defined by rows of pits, constructed perhaps for a mixture of economic and ritual activities. Elaborate long mounds or barrows were built for the burial of the dead, or at least for those who were socially important. Fifteen possible examples have been found recently in Suffolk by means of aerial photography. Other monuments of a supposedly religious kind which appear for the first time are processional avenues or 'cursuses', as at Fornham All Saints and Stratford St Mary. Both these sites also contain circular enclosures with complicated internal features, sunken or standing, which are akin to the temples or 'henge-monuments' of southern England.

In the succeeding Bronze Age, the technological armoury was further improved by the discovery of metallurgy. Copper, tin, gold, silver and particularly bronze (an alloy of copper and tin) were all worked for the manufacture of ornaments, tools and weapons. Large numbers of early metal artefacts have been found in Suffolk including swords, spearheads and axes of various kinds. Some were found in hoards, and probably represent the property of tinkers or metalsmiths who buried them for safety's sake.

Several contemporary settlements have been identified in the county, for example at Lakenheath and Sutton Hoo. They normally appear as patterns of hearths, scoops and pits, but at West Row, Mildenhall, Edward Martin has recently uncovered a Bronze-Age house—the first to be recorded in Suffolk. It is a circular post-built structure 16½ feet in diameter, with a porch facing south-east. Its occupants used large amounts of pottery, worked flint, grew cereals and processed flax.

The most important field-monument of the Bronze Age is undoubtedly the round barrow. About 110 of these burial mounds still survive above ground, particularly on the Breckland and Sandlings where much heathland remained unploughed until the 19th century. Many more have been destroyed over the centuries by local ploughmen, but fortunately aerial reconnaissance has re-discovered about 500 of them as 'ring-ditches'. The mounds have been ploughed flat but the surrounding ditches, though filled in, still show as distinct crop-marks (illus. 10). Together, ring-ditches and surviving mounds give the best indication of how the prehistoric population of Suffolk was distributed—certainly in death and probably in life (illus. 8). The main concentrations were on the Breckland, the chalk downland around Newmarket and the Sandlings of the east coast (particularly on the Felixstowe and Shotley peninsulas). While the centre of the county produces only a few burial-sites, the gravel terraces of certain river valleys such as the Gipping, Brett and Stour were obviously well populated. From the human remains in barrows and flat graves, it has been shown that the average male in Bronze Age Suffolk was 5 feet 7½ inches tall and died aged 34; the average female was 5 feet 4 inches tall and was 37½ when she died.

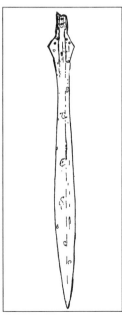

7 *Bronze-Age sword, probably seventh century B.C., found at Brandon. Note holes and rivets.*

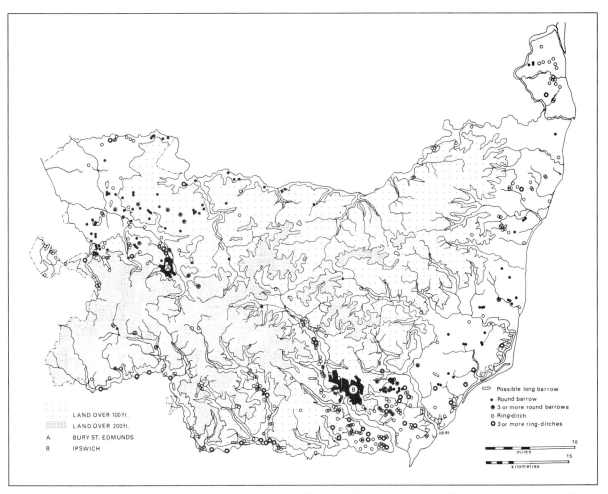

8 *Prehistorical burial mounds in Suffolk showing those still visible above ground, and flattened mounds whose ditches have been recovered by aerial photography. The main concentrations avoid the heaviest, most forested land in the centre of the county.*

In parts of the Felixstowe peninsula, round barrows are on, or very close to, parish boundaries. Good examples can be seen on the boundaries of Nacton, Foxhall and Bucklesham. This relationship, which also appears on the Breckland, suggests that *some* of our modern boundaries may have descended from economic units or estates which existed in the second or first millennium B.C.

In the last 650 years B.C., local people acquired the use of iron, a much harder metal than bronze. Unfortunately, iron rusts in the ground and survivals, like the sword found in 1913 at Lakenheath, are rare. For decorative purposes, however, softer metals such as bronze and gold remained in common use. The best local example must be the six decorative collars or 'torcs' found at Ipswich in 1968-70, 'the richest Iron Age hoard yet found in England'. These beautiful objects of the first century B.C. are made of gold mixed with a little silver. Each collar is made of two or four rods twisted together while most of the finials carry

9 *Barbed and tanged flint arrowhead, Bronze Age, found on Breckland.*

10 *Shottisham: buried landscapes of prehistoric and Roman times seen from the air—ploughed-out barrows or ring-ditches, roads and field-boundaries.*

11 *Decorated finial of gold torc, first century B.C., found at Ipswich.*

embossed spiral decorations. The hoard was probably the property of a travelling goldsmith, because the surfaces of the torcs are still rough and unfinished.

Until the 1960s, most archaeologists had difficulty in recognising Iron-Age pottery and ordinary farming settlements. Now such evidence is being found regularly and a few sites have already been excavated. For instance, in 1979 a circular post-built house was uncovered, associated with two furnaces or ovens on a hill-top at Barham. A similar unenclosed farmstead with round houses, pits and ditches was excavated at West Stow, stratified beneath an Anglo-Saxon village.

No fields of the Iron Age have been positively identified in Suffolk, though many must have existed. The first proven examples may come from extensive ditched systems now being discovered on aerial photographs, especially on the Shotley and Felixstowe peninsulas, or from new work at Yaxley where the alignment of fields and tracks completely ignores a major Roman road and may therefore be earlier than the road. Already, palaeobotanists working at Old Buckenham Mere in South Norfolk have shown that the heavy lands of central East Anglia underwent their 'first substantial clearance' in the Iron Age and Roman period. The pollens of trees declined rapidly as those of herbaceous species, typical of grassland, increased.

The concern with warfare first seen in military weapons of the Bronze Age, certainly grew in the Iron Age. East Anglia does not have many 'hill-forts' so typical of the period in other parts of Britain, but two certain examples have been identified in Suffolk. At Barnham, a small fort of the second-first century B.C., measuring 105 by 77 yards, was surrounded by double ramparts and ditches. On excavation the ditches were found to be 23 feet wide by 10 feet deep. Around the churchyard at Burgh is a larger rectangular earthwork measuring 300 by 225 yards. It too was defended by a double bank and ditch, and has yielded pottery of the first centuries B.C. and A.D. Society was clearly becoming more hierarchical, presided over by a military aristocracy who had the wealth to commission luxury goods like the Ipswich torcs. Population was probably rising, and political boundaries were being drawn and defended as never before.

An important political and military boundary seems to have run across Suffolk in the later Iron Age. The Trinovantes were a Celtic tribe who lived where Essex is today, but early in the first century A.D. they were conquered by their powerful western neighbours called the Catuvellauni. Together they

12 *Bildeston: line of Roman road marked by a track, hedge and parish-boundary.*

were ruled by King Cunobelinus (Shakespeare's Cymbeline). The distribution of coins and other artefacts suggests that the south of Suffolk was also absorbed into Cunobelinus' empire. The fort at Burgh may previously have been the centre of a small independent territory stretching from the Alde to the Gipping, but it was probably taken by the Trinovantes before they, in turn, were conquered by the Catuvellauni. Coin-evidence also shows that the whole of modern Norfolk and the Breckland part of Suffolk, down to modern Bury were inhabited by the Iceni. The boundary between the two kingdoms seems to have run approximately from Newmarket in the west to Aldeburgh in the east, following the natural watershed which meanders across the heavy, forested clay of central Suffolk. This, after all, was a cultural boundary which was already thousands of years old. For example, the distribution of Neolithic axes and Bronze-Age burials had shown similar concentrations in the south-east and north-west, divided by the central forests which were difficult to penetrate and colonise.

Four centuries of Roman rule (illus. 16)

The conquest of Britain began in A.D. 43 when four legions and auxiliary troops landed in Kent and fought their way to the Thames. Thereafter under the command of the Emperor Claudius himself, the army defeated the Catuvellauni, the most powerful of British tribes, and captured their ramparted stronghold of *Camulodunum*. On a nearby ridge, the Romans soon began to build their own town, now Colchester, which, with its great temple dedicated to Claudius, became the first capital of the new Roman province of Britannia.

The Iceni welcomed the downfall of their aggressive Catuvellaunian neighbours, and signed a treaty of friendship with Rome. This gave them a measure of self government, while it gave the Romans a secure right flank for their advance into the midlands and north. The arrangement was shaky at times (in A.D. 47 the Iceni joined a rebellion and were subdued by military force) but it preserved some independence for the region for 17 years—until the dramatic events of A.D. 61.

The rebellion of Boudicca is the first major incident of regional history to be recorded in documentary form, principally in the Latin writings of Tacitus and Dio Cassius. When Prasutagus, client-king of the Iceni, died during the winter of A.D. 60/61, the Romans began to exert pressure by revoking grants and interfering with the king's bequests. When the king's widow, Boudicca, was whipped and her daughters raped, the Iceni blazed into armed rebellion and persuaded

13 *Walton Castle: the remains of a major Roman fort of the third to fourth centuries A.D., near Felixstowe. These lumps of masonry had fallen from the cliff-top; at low tide, fragments are still visible today. Engravings published in 1786.*

their southern neighbours, the Trinovantes, to join them. Thus united, the native population of the east turned its rage on the nearest great symbol of Roman civilisation, *Camulodunum*. After a two-day siege, they sacked the town and slaughtered its inhabitants. Hearing of the rebellion, the IXth Legion marched south from its base in the Nene valley but, too late to save *Camulodunum*, was ambushed by the rebels and lost at least 1,000 men. This engagement may have taken place in the wooded Stour valley near modern Haverhill.

14 *Icenian silver coin of first century A.D.: prancing horse with letters ECE.*

The rebels went on to sack the major towns of London and *Verulamium* near modern St Albans. Their inhabitants were murdered by 'gibbet, fire and cross'. Faced with this deepening crisis which could have driven the Romans off the island, the governor of Britain, Paulinus, gathered as many troops as he could in a well-chosen position somewhere in the midlands. His army of barely 10,000 men faced a British horde about ten times larger. With their superior discipline and equipment, the Romans withstood a frenzied attack and then cut their way to victory, slaughtering thousands of the rebels as they fled in confusion. Boudicca died soon after the final battle, in mysterious circumstances, while the Iceni were absorbed into the Roman province and felt the full force of Paulinus' revenge. Later, as more conciliatory policies were pursued the region steadily recovered and acquired the usual trappings of Roman culture.

An accidental find in Suffolk provides a remarkable illustration of the bloody and tragic events of A.D. 61. In 1907 a boy swimming in the river Alde at Rendham fished out a life-size bronze head of the Emperor Claudius. Now in the British Museum, this head appears to have been violently hacked from a large statue. It was probably looted from *Camulodunum*, brought back in triumph but later thrown into the river by a native anxious to escape retribution.

The east of Britain, like other areas, was at first controlled by a strategic network of Roman roads and forts. In the south of Suffolk, forts were probably built when Claudius defeated the Catuvellaunian occupiers of Trinovantian territory: Coddenham and Long Melford are likely places. The rest of the system dates from the forcible subjection of the Iceni after A.D. 61. For example, the two main north-south roads of Roman Suffolk were certainly military in origin. They are Pye Street which is basically the Ipswich-Norwich road of today, and the Peddars Way which links Melford, Ixworth and Knettishall. A typical Roman fort of seven acres at Pakenham, defended by triple ditches, commanded the ford where the Peddars Way crossed the river Blackbourn, while at Stuston near Eye aerial photographs have revealed what may be the outline of a temporary marching camp.

15 *Bronze head of Emperor Claudius found in river Alde at Rendham. Probably looted from Colchester in Boudicca's revolt.*

Though they can sometimes be confused with enclosure roads of the period 1150-1850, about 400 miles of Roman roads still stand out on the modern map of Suffolk. For example, the A1120 from Pettaugh to Peasenhall is noticeably straight for about 12 miles in an area of winding lanes, and is part of a Roman road which ran from the Gipping valley to the east coast near Dunwich. Elsewhere, roads of this period can only be pieced together by lining up hedges, parish boundaries, minor tracks and soil marks. A good example runs from Melford eastwards through Brent Eleigh and Wattisham. Nearly all the Roman roads recorded by the Ordnance Survey were major routes linking important

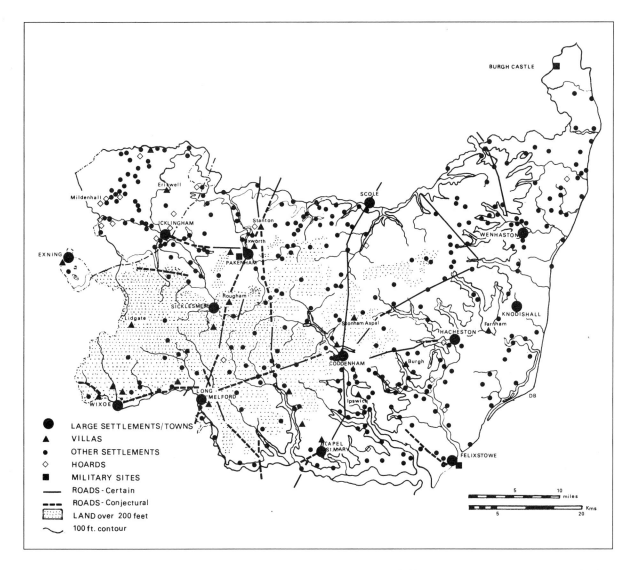

16 *Roman Suffolk: large numbers of rural farmsteads and villages have been recently discovered. Empty areas on the map undoubtedly contain other examples, as yet unfound by aerial reconnaisance and fieldwork.*

settlements, yet even they are only partially reconstructed or have missing lengths. We know very little of the huge network of minor roads which served individual villages, farms and fields—except in favoured areas like the Shotley peninsula where such features are visible from the air.

Within Suffolk the Romans built no walled towns with sophisticated features like fora and amphitheatres. Nevertheless, archaeologists have recently identified several undefended towns, which sprawl in an apparently unplanned way but certainly had commercial and industrial importance. Hacheston, for example, has produced the outlines of timber buildings, roads, numerous rubbish pits, hearths for working metal and pottery kilns. In a similar way, the Roman town of Icklingham, which was probably called *Camboritum*, sprawled for half a mile along the valley side, and contained several pottery kilns and some buildings of quality with tiled floors. Such communities resembled the market towns and manufacturing centres of medieval times, each serving a scattered rural population.

Villas are another clear symbol of Romanisation. They were large and substantially built farmhouses owned by major landowners. Although only a few have been excavated, mostly inadequately, the sites of a score or more villas have been mapped in Suffolk, scattered fairly widely on both light and heavy land. Although they varied in sophistication, some were expressions of considerable personal wealth; at Whitton near Ipswich a large villa had several tesselated pavements, while another at Stonham Aspal had a bath house with painted plaster and under-floor heating. Aerial photography has recently revealed the complete plan of a corridor-villa at Lidgate. It consisted of a main range with two side wings, and was subdivided into more than 20 rooms. A few yards away was a large buttressed barn for the owner's grain.

In recent years, the most important development in the archaeology of this period has been the discovery of large numbers of minor rural settlements often coincident with earlier Iron Age sites. Occasional excavation has been done, for instance at Wangford near Lakenheath where a round hut of timber with a clay floor was uncovered, and at Hadleigh where a rectangular enclosure yielded shallow ditches and roof tiles. In most cases, however, the sites have been discovered from pottery and other domestic debris scattered on the surface of ploughed land. When large areas are systematically searched by the new technique of 'field-walking', the density of Roman sites often turns out to be surprisingly high. For example, at Mendlesham the Colchester family searched all the available land in a parish of about 4,000 acres. They discovered 15 Romano-British sites in an area which archaeologists used to regard as uncolonised. Most of the sites lay on the east side of the parish near a major Roman road; they yielded small scatters of pottery, and probably represent no more than isolated farms. One site, however, covered two acres and appears to be the remains of a hamlet with several households. Field-walking in other parishes on heavy clay land, such as Walsham-le-Willows and Metfield, has produced similar results (illus. 18). All this work implies that the Romano-British population was much higher than used to be thought, and that virtually all kinds of land were being settled.

It is important to remember that native farmsteads and villages were originally surrounded by fields and pastures. In those parishes which have been systematically searched, the number of habitations implies that considerable areas were being cleared and farmed. Even on heavy land the damp oak-forest must have contained frequent clearances hacked by a numerous and increasing population. Only a few field-systems have been excavated, though with interesting results: at Hacheston, for example, ditches were uncovered in a rectilinear pattern of small fields. Aerial photography is also revealing patterns of early fields, in particular on sandy and gravelly soils and many of them are likely to be Romano-British in date.

When faced with political or military uncertainty, people were often tempted to bury their most precious possessions. Thus from the late second century

17 *Bastion of Roman fortress at Burgh Castle, late third century A.D. The walls still stand 15 feet high and enclose six acres.*

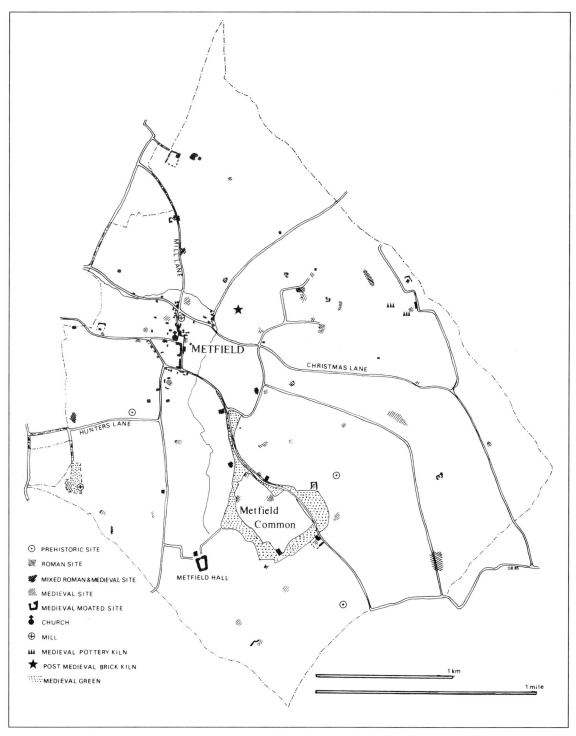

18 *Settlement History of a Suffolk Parish: Michael Hardy's systematic field-walking of Metfield has shown the high density of Roman and medieval settlements, and the ever-changing pattern of human occupation.*

onwards, under the threat of revolts, civil war and invasion, large collections of coin were frequently put into the ground. One of the most impressive of Suffolk's hoards is the so-called Mildenhall Treasure. Thirty-four objects of almost pure silver had been buried in the later fourth century: they included dishes, bowls, goblets, ladles and spoons. Some of the silver was decorated with figures of pagan gods, nereids, satyrs and nymphs, in varying attitudes of Bacchic revelry. Yet three of the spoons bear Christian symbols. Considerable uncertainty remains as to the interpretation of this fabulous treasure—the places of manufacture, probably on the continent, cannot yet be recognised—and it is not known whether the owner was a wealthy person who lived locally, or someone who was merely passing through; nor finally, is it understood why the hoard contains a mixture of Christian and blatantly pagan objects. In 1992 another extraordinary hoard was excavated at Hoxne. It had been buried in a wooden box in the early years of the fifth century, and consisted of nearly 15,000 coins; tableware of silver including 78 spoons and a handle in the shape of a leaping tigress; and 29 pieces of gold jewellery including a body-chain. This hoard too displayed Christian inscriptions, as well as seven personal names.

The best evidence that Christianity, made official by the Emperor Constantine in A.D. 313, took root in this remote part of the Empire comes from Icklingham. Over several generations, the Roman town has produced four lead tanks bearing the familiar Christian symbols of chi-rho, alpha and omega. In 1974, excavation near the spot where one of the tanks was found revealed an apparently Christian cemetery. It contained skeletons orientated west-east and the fragmentary outlines of several buildings. One building enclosed a small apsed bath which, from continental parallels, was almost certainly a Christian font or baptistry, while another rectangular building has been interpreted as a church. The tanks themselves had presumably been used for some liturgical purpose, such as ritual washing. This evidence for all its deficiencies, enables us to descry a Christian community worshipping in Suffolk only three centuries after the death of Christ.

In the later third century a system of defences was built along the coasts of Britain to repulse the raids of Germanic pirates from across the North Sea. The system, known as the Saxon Shore, depended on a string of heavily defended bases from which ships and men could be sent out to intercept raiders by sea or land. Two of these bases were built in Suffolk. One was on the cliffs at Walton near Felixstowe but it has been undermined by the sea and only small hunks of masonry are now visible at low tide (illus. 13). At Burgh Castle or *Gariannonum*, three sides of a massive fortress survive beside the river Waveney. The flint and brick walls still stand 15 feet high, with six solid bastions which originally carried *ballistae* or spring-guns. Although it was breached in A.D. 367, the Saxon Shore survived for more than a century, but the Roman province was increasingly on the defensive and the barbarians could not be kept at bay for ever.

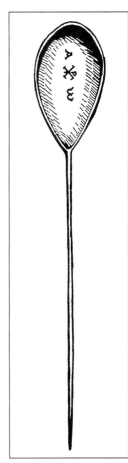

19 *Silver spoon with Christian symbols, from the Mildenhall Treasure buried in the late fourth century A.D.*

2

The South Folk of the East Angles

20 *Small gold plaque of the ninth century found at Brandon in 1978. It depicts St John the Evangelist.*

At this period we can, for the first time, talk legitimately of Suffolk. The word applies to those 'folk' who lived at the southern end of the new Anglo-Saxon kingdom of East Anglia. The boundaries of this folk-area were broadly defined by two major valleys. To the north, the double valley of the Waveney and Little Ouse divided Suffolk from the related 'North Folk', while to the south the Stour divided it from the kingdom of Essex, the East Saxons. Although the name Suffolk is first recorded in a document of *c.*1045, it was surely current much earlier.

The Anglo-Saxon period presents considerable historical difficulties. First, it is over 600 years long (the same length of time by which we are separated from the Peasants' Revolt of the 14th century). Secondly, the evidence is varied, scanty and difficult to interpret. Any reconstruction has to rely on archaeological excavation and fieldwork, reinforced by the study of place-names, buildings and a few documents. Nevertheless, the period is less 'dark' than it used to be, because of major achievements since about 1960.

Who were the East Angles, who migrated to this region and settled it from the fifth to the seventh centuries? They appear to have been a mixed Germanic population who included Saxons, Frisians and some Franks, but were under the control of Angles. They came from various parts of northern Europe, from the Jutland peninsula, northern Germany and modern Holland. Their cemeteries have been found in large numbers and form the greater part of our archaeological evidence for the early period. Being true to their native gods, they buried their dead with grave-goods, ranging from domestic pottery to weapons. These hint at interesting social differences. For example, a few men were buried with swords while a larger number had spears; on the other hand, many burials had no weapons at all. These pagan cemeteries are found mainly at the western and eastern ends of Suffolk, and are related to estuaries and rivers flowing either into the Wash or into the North Sea. One of the best studied is at Lackford in the Lark valley, where a large cemetery of the sixth century occupies a sandy spur just above the river. At least 1,000 cremations in globular urns, accompanied by numerous brooches, combs and personal objects, lie beside a large Roman settlement.

Archaeologists are now beginning to find the dwellings of these pagan people, and the emphasis has swung from how they died to how they lived. At West Stow on the Breckland, a pagan village of national and international importance was excavated by Stanley West in the years 1965-72. It is sited on a small sandy hillock beside the river Lark, and was occupied from the fifth to the early seventh century. Its accompanying cemetery, about 400 yards away, had been found in the 19th century. The most common buildings on the site were over 70 small timber huts constructed over excavated pits. The huts appear to have been used variously for storage, domestic industries like weaving, and for living accommodation. For every seven to ten small huts, there was a larger hall which West interprets as the main dwelling of a family. The village apparently consisted of three or four extended families who eventually defined their properties by digging ditches. So far, all the pagan settlements which have been identified lie on the lighter soils of the Breckland and Sandlings, and they all appear to have been abandoned in the seventh century as families drifted away one by one. This certainly suggests a major change of life-style, which may be connected with the acceptance of Christianity.

But while the new immigrants established themselves in Suffolk, what was happening to the native Romano-Britons? The traditional view was that, once the military and political system of the Roman province collapsed, most of them were either killed or fled to the west. No longer does this seem feasible, and it is currently assumed that an appreciable number of Celtic people survived but fell increasingly under the control of the invaders.

This change of interpretation depends on the following arguments. First, although the total population may have declined seriously as the result of warfare and disease, the sheer number of Romano-British settlements in every part of Suffolk makes it extremely unlikely that all the natives were exterminated or driven out. One of the best resources available to the conquerors was an established labour-force on organised estates which were still capable of being farmed. It made no sense to destroy this agrarian economy, any more than was absolutely necessary to take control. Secondly, certain linear earthworks such as the Black Ditches on Cavenham Heath or the War Banks at Lawshall may represent defences across the Roman roads, thrown up by British communities holding out temporarily against the invaders. Thirdly, it is possible to exaggerate the numbers of immigrants. In fact, the Anglo-Saxons built up their population slowly over two to three centuries; each cemetery therefore contains several generations, drawn perhaps from more than one village.

The argument about British survival is no more than the balancing of possibilities, and is complicated by the archaeological 'invisibility' of the Romano-Britons from the early fifth century onwards. Nearly all their settlements were abandoned sooner or later, but they themselves could have survived in some numbers. Whatever the relative balance of the two races, British and Germanic, there is little doubt that the latter took total political and military control. The dominance of Anglo-Saxon place-names, often incorporating the name of the 'head man', is one of the striking legacies of the period on our modern map.

21 *Ceremonial whetstone or sceptre, 2 feet 9½ inches long, from ship-burial at Sutton Hoo.*

A new kingdom and religion

By about A.D. 550, the conquest was complete and a new united kingdom had emerged, known as East Anglia. The ruling family, who significantly claimed descent from both Woden *and* Caesar, were called the Wuffingas. According to the Venerable Bede, their most distinguished king was Redwald who ruled from

22 *The Anglo-Saxon ship at Sutton Hoo, as excavated in 1939.*

599 to 624/5. He was eventually acknowledged as overlord by other English kings and helped to depose a king of Northumbria. Redwald's successors were less accomplished; four of them died in battle, and East Anglia became increasingly dominated by more powerful neighbours, particularly the Mercians. The famous Devil's Ditch across Newmarket Heath is almost certainly a boundary of East Anglia, established in the sixth or seventh century, to guard the main landward approach from the west and south-west (illus. 24).

The main seat of the Wuffingas was, we are told by Bede, at Rendlesham. This, curiously, is in the extreme south-eastern corner of the kingdom, and presumably represents the original home of the family and their early sphere of influence. Nearby at Sutton Hoo, on a bluff overlooking the river Deben, lay a cemetery of about 15 earthen mounds. Here, in 1939, the famous ship-burial was unearthed. A wooden ship, 80 feet long and 14 feet wide with places for 38 oarsmen, had been hauled up from the Deben and lowered into a rectangular pit. In a cabin amidships were the traces of a human burial accompanied by the magnificent treasure which can now be seen in the British Museum. It contains antique silver from eastern Europe, late classical spoons and magnificent goldwork by East Anglian craftsmen. The latest opinion is that the burial was for Redwald himself. Sutton Hoo provides a wonderfully instructive contrast to West Stow: the latter reveals the lives of peasant farmers who must have existed all over the region and provided an essential base for the economy, while the former represents the political power and wealth of a ruling class, able to commission the finest craftsmanship of the day.

Another vital theme of Anglo-Saxon history is the adoption of Christianity. On a visit to King Ethelbert of Kent, Redwald was persuaded to introduce Christianity into East Anglia, but he did so in a half-hearted way. In his hall at Rendlesham, he set up his Christian altar beside a pagan one—trying to serve both Christ and the ancient gods. After another period of heathenism, his son Sigebert proved a far more committed Christian. He founded a monastery at Bedricsworth (later Bury St Edmunds) to which he retired, and invited two important figures into the kingdom. The first was St Felix, a Burgundian, who became the first bishop of the East Angles with his seat at *Domnoc* (usually interpreted as Dunwich, though Felixstowe has also been suggested). The second was St Fursey, an Irish monk and mystic who built a monastery on a site given by the king, in the old Roman fort at Burgh Castle. Charles Green's excavations in the 1960s revealed parts of Fursey's primitive monastery. Thus, East Anglia had representatives of both the Roman and Celtic forms of Christianity.

From the death of Felix until the Danish Conquest of 869, the bishops of East Anglia encouraged the foundation and building of new monasteries and churches. Missionary churches or 'minsters' were established at places like Sudbury and Bury St Edmunds, while dedications to saints such as Gregory, Helen and Ethelbert (an East Anglian king martyred in the eighth century) may well indicate churches founded before the Danish invasion. Particularly influential was a monastery founded in 654 by St Botolph, 'a man of unparalleled life and learning'. It lay at a place called *Icanho*, which can now be confidently identified as Iken, a remote spur overlooking the Alde estuary. Here in 1977 Stanley West found a

23 *Helmet from ship burial at Sutton Hoo, restored.*

24 *The Devil's Ditch near Newmarket: a massive rampart and ditch, 7¼ miles long, commanding the chalk ridge which forms a natural entry to the region. Probably fifth to seventh century A.D., part of the boundary of the Anglo-Saxon kingdom and diocese of East Anglia.*

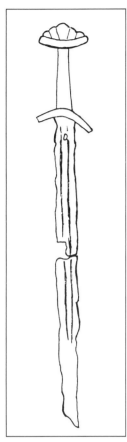

25 *Iron sword of Viking type, 10th century, found at Saxtead Green.*

26 *The wolf finding St Edmund's head: bench-end from Hadleigh church.*

commemorative cross-shaft of about 900, and excavated a timber-framed building of Middle Saxon date, underlying the present Norman church.

St Edmund and the Danes

The most important incident connected with Suffolk's early Christianity is undoubtedly the martyrdom of St Edmund in 869. Edmund was king of East Anglia but little is known about his reign—except its end. When his kingdom was attacked by a Danish army, he reluctantly led his forces into battle at a place called 'Haegelisdun' and was defeated. He was taken prisoner, cruelly put to death, and buried nearby at 'Sutton'. Several claims have been made about the identity of these places: for example, that Hellesdon near Norwich was the scene of the battle, and that the burial place is Sutton near Sutton Hoo. Furthermore, the inhabitants of Hoxne have believed since the early Middle Ages that Edmund was martyred there. However, a new theory advanced by Stanley West seems the most acceptable of all. In the parish of Bradfield St Clare, he has found a field called 'Hellesden'. One mile to the south is Sutton Hall. Both places are within five miles of Bury, to which the sacred body was moved in the early 10th century.

Well within living memory of Edmund's death, special memorial coins were being struck and were circulating widely in eastern England. Furthermore, within two generations of his death, he was accepted as a saint. The cult of St Edmund grew very quickly, not just because he died a saintly death but also because he was a patriotic hero who symbolised East Anglian 'resistance' to Danish oppression.

The Danes had begun to attack eastern England in 841 and, after the defeat of Edmund and his army, they 'shared out the land' of East Anglia. Unfortunately, the size of their army is not known, nor is the size of the civilian population which undoubtedly followed them from Scandinavia. The impact of the Danes on place-names was certainly not very great, apart from a few suffixes like *-by* and *-thorpe*. However, two things are certain: the Danes formed, for a time at least, yet another aristocracy imposed by conquest on native society, and they were fairly quickly absorbed. Guthrum, the first Danish king of East Anglia, who is said to have been buried in 890 at Hadleigh, became Christian and was a godson of King Alfred of Wessex. In 917, after a bloody siege at Colchester, East Anglia was rapidly re-conquered by Edward the Elder and the Danish army of East Anglia capitulated and gave allegiance to him. From this time onwards, East Anglia was absorbed into the kingdom of England, united under the crown of Wessex.

Country and town

Meanwhile, from the seventh century onwards, the landscape had changed in two significant ways. First, the old 'pagan' settlements appear to have been abandoned in favour of new sites which usually show a much closer association with medieval and modern villages. Thus, pottery of the Middle and Late Saxon periods has been found in the present village of West Stow, over a mile from the 'pagan' village. At Brandon, beside the Little Ouse, one of the most impor-

I *Dunwich: view north along coast towards Southwold. The shingle bank blocks the remains of the medieval harbour of this once major port.*

II *Westleton: surviving relic of the typical heathland of the Sandlings, for long grazed by sheep and now invaded by scrub.*

III *Stoke by Nayland: the typical building materials of East Anglia.*

IV *Burgh Castle: Roman fort guarding Breydon Water and surrounding marshland.*

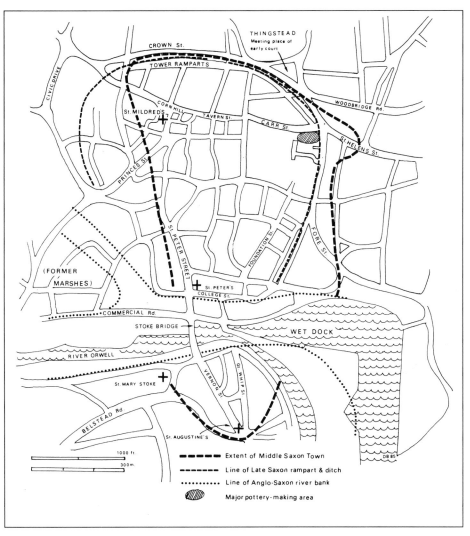

27 *Anglo-Saxon Ipswich: recent discoveries have established the large size of this industrialised town of A.D. 650-850. The churches marked were possibly founded in that period.*

tant Middle Saxon sites in England, has been excavated by Bob Carr. It lies on a sandy island, and was occupied from the seventh to ninth centuries. It consisted of sophisticated timber buildings, one of which was aisled and another is probably a church. Normal construction was of close-set planks, occasionally set in shallow trenches. In some cases, post-holes contained actual wood which can be scientifically examined. The excavators have found considerable numbers of artefacts, including abundant 'Ipswich Ware', Merovingian pottery imported from the continent, coins, and a gold plaque inscribed with the eagle and name of St John the Evangelist. Indeed, so spectacular are the finds that the site can hardly be accepted as an ordinary village; it may be an aristocratic establishment or a religious community.

The other major feature is the sudden appearance of Ipswich as a town, indeed as the first known town in Britain since the Roman period. It was thriving

28 *Debenham: tower with Anglo-Saxon long-and-short work.*

commercially and industrially long before the emergence of Thetford, Dunwich or Norwich. Excavations and chance finds have shown that the Middle-Saxon town covered 125 acres—which is 50 times bigger than the average contemporary village and roughly the same size as the later medieval town of Ipswich (illus. 27). It is now claimed by Keith Wade as 'the largest known early trading community in north-west Europe'. Its inhabitants were dealing with Belgium, Holland and the Rhineland, as well as practising the crafts of weaving, fishing, metal-working and, above all, the making of a distinctive, if uninspiring, pottery which was sold widely over eastern England. Such rapid economic development strongly suggests that the town was under the special patronage and control of the East Anglian kings, whose palace was at nearby Rendlesham.

Anglo-Danish Suffolk

In the late Saxon period, historical sources are more numerous, and tell us in greater detail of political and military events. Towards the end of the 10th century a second wave of Danish attacks assailed East Anglia. In 991, Olaf landed with 93 ships, over-ran Ipswich and defeated Ealdorman Brihtnoth at the celebrated battle of Maldon. In 1010 Ipswich again suffered, this time at the hands of Thorkel. The heroic efforts of Ulfketel, earl of East Anglia, were unavailing, for in 1016 King Edmund of Wessex was decisively defeated by Canute at Ashingdon in Essex and 'all the nobility of England were there destroyed', including Ulfketel himself. Canute assumed the crown, and for a time Suffolk, and England, became part of a large Scandinavian empire.

Meanwhile, life in the countryside was changing significantly. A steady growth of population meant that villages were expanding, new virgin sites were being occupied, the land was being intensively farmed, and large parishes were frequently subdivided into smaller units (hence, for example, the frequent Magnas and Parvas mentioned in Domesday Book). At the same time, the church made a speedy recovery from the ravages of the first Danish invasions. The bishopric of East Anglia was restored in the early 10th century, monastic life was revived at Bury St Edmunds and, above all, new parish churches were founded all over the county by lay lords and groups of freemen. Norman Scarfe has shown, from Domesday Book, that four-fifths of the medieval churches of Suffolk were already in existence by the time of the Norman Conquest. In some cases, the partial fabric of these early churches still survives, as at Claydon, Debenham and Fakenham Magna.

Also, by the 11th century, at least 10 places other than Ipswich were acquiring some kind of urban status. Domesday Book records markets at Thorney (Stowmarket), Kelsale, Beccles, Hoxne, Eye, Clare and Haverhill. Six places already contained burgesses, which means that their inhabitants had acquired political and commercial privileges from their lords. These towns were Ipswich, which by this time had a mint; Dunwich, which is the only coastal port; Eye, Beccles, Clare, and Sudbury. Bury St Edmunds had also developed commercially after the cult of St Edmund took root in the early 10th century, and had acquired its present name before the Norman Conquest.

3

The Normans and English, 1066-1300

The Norman Conquest is often seen as a total break in English history. In fact, it represents the take-over by yet another dynasty and aristocracy, amounting perhaps to fewer than 5,000 people, while beneath them English society survived relatively unchanged. Hence Domesday Book, compiled in 1086, must not be seen as simply a survey of Norman England, but also as a stocktaking of centuries of Anglo-Saxon history. After the anarchy of the early 11th century, and the weak reigns of Ethelred the Unready and Edward the Confessor, the highly organised and ruthless rule of William I and his henchmen promised much greater stability. Nevertheless, the early years of the Conquest were by no means peaceful. A Danish force invaded East Anglia in 1069 and had to be defeated near Ipswich. In addition, the first Norman earl of East Anglia, Ralph Wader, plotted rebellion while celebrating his marriage at Exning, in 1076, and was subsequently defeated and outlawed.

29 *Initial from 12th-century book of sermons owned by Bury Abbey.*

By 1086, Domesday Book reveals 71 tenants-in-chief in Suffolk (of whom 21 held lands in Norfolk and Essex as well). Very few English people were mentioned, except in very minor positions, and the vast majority were Norman-French. Naturally, the king himself heads the list. His estates included the major town of Ipswich, nearly all the Hundred of Lothingland and important areas in the Hundred of Samford. After him comes a long list of lay barons like Robert of Mortain who was half-brother to the king, Count Alan of Brittany who took over much of Earl Ralph's possessions, and William de Warenne who also had major estates in Norfolk and Sussex. But three other names are outstanding for the size and importance of their holdings in Suffolk.

Richard de Clare, son of Count Gilbert de Brionne, was chief justice and confidant of the Conqueror, and helped to suppress the revolt of 1076. He was granted 170 different lordships in England, of which 95 were in Suffolk. The castle and borough of Clare became the centre of a great 'Honour' or scattered estate, and the family throughout the Middle Ages was known as Fitzgilbert or de Clare. Similarly Roger Bigod received 117 manors in Suffolk. His descendants became Earls of Norfolk in the 12th century, and administered their estates from four castles, at Ipswich, Bungay, Walton and Framlingham. Hugh Bigod, the first earl, rebelled twice against Henry II, but the family survived until the fifth earl was deprived of his estates by Edward I. The third great Norman magnate was William Malet, who received no fewer than 221 holdings in Suffolk, including most of the lands of Edric of Laxfield. His main residence was the castle and borough of Eye, the estate being known as the Honour of

35

30 *The 'Bury Cross' now in Metropolitan Museum in New York: detail showing the Ascension. Second quarter of the 12th century.*

Eye. When, in 1110, his son Robert plotted against the king and was banished, the castle and Honour were taken into royal hands.

Already by 1086, a high proportion of Suffolk was owned by the church. For example, the great Benedictine abbey of Ely held several manors scattered around the county, including Lakenheath, Glemsford and Wetheringsett, but its main centre of influence was in the south-east around Woodbridge. There, it not only owned certain manors but the jurisdiction of five-and-a-half Hundreds known as the Liberty of St Etheldreda or the 'Wicklaw'—an area which functioned almost as a separate administrative 'shire' until 1889. Other religious owners were Lanfranc, the Archbishop of Canterbury, the French Bishops of Bayeux and Evreux, and the English Bishops of Rochester and Thetford. Monastic owners included the abbeys of Ramsey, Bernai and Chatteris. But they were all dwarfed by the Abbey of Bury, which had about 300 separate holdings in Suffolk, Norfolk, Essex and elsewhere. About 70 of them lay in the western half of Suffolk and included the specially valuable manors of Mildenhall and Melford, and almost the whole of the Hundreds of Thingoe and Blackbourn. In 1044 Edward the Confessor had given to the abbey jurisdiction over the eight-and-a-half Hundreds of western Suffolk, known as the Liberty of St Edmund. This privilege, similar to Ely's control of the Wicklaw, is the origin of West Suffolk's administrative independence which survived until 1974.

Castles are the most enduring symbols of the Norman Conquest. About 20 were built in Suffolk by various Norman lords, either in large strategic towns such as Ipswich and Thetford, or at the centres of personal and feudal estates as at Clare and Framlingham. Built either in the form of 'ringworks' or 'mottes and baileys', they consisted of earthen mounds, banks and ditches, probably at first with timber buildings and palisades. A fine example of a Norman earthwork castle with two baileys still survives at Haughley, originally the seat of Hugh de Montfort. At a later stage castles were often rebuilt more solidly in stone, and could be substantially remodelled or extended. Some of the smaller earthworks, as at Offton and Milden, may be 'adulterine' defences thrown up unofficially during the civil war between Stephen and Matilda. The best documented of Suffolk's early castles is Orford which Henry II built between 1165 and 1173 with a tall polygonal keep—at a total cost of £1,413. Suffolk's castles were not simply residences and symbols of power for, on occasions, they were attacked, captured and even dismantled. For example, when King Henry II's eldest son rebelled in 1173, he was supported by a mercenary army, commanded by the Earl of Leicester, which landed on the Suffolk coast. Leicester first attacked the ramparts of Dunwich, was repulsed and then attempted, unsuccessfully, to take the castle at Walton. When the rebels reached Framlingham, Hugh Bigod threw in his lot with Leicester, and the two earls proceeded westwards across Suffolk, committing various atrocities on the way. At Fornham near Bury, they met a royal army led by Richard de Lucy and were decisively beaten. Bigod escaped but was later cornered by royal troops: he then made his peace with the king and paid a heavy fine. At Bungay castle, a tunnel where the royal attackers had started to undermine the keep still survives. After the surrender, this castle and the two other Bigod strongholds at Framlingham and

31 *Orford Castle: keep built by Henry II in 1165-67.*

Walton were demolished on the king's orders. Ironically, less than 20 years later, Richard I gave permission to Hugh's son, Roger, to rebuild Framlingham. Following the latest ideas in military planning, Roger constructed the present castle, with its tall curtain wall and 13 projecting towers (illus. 32). Sixteen years after its completion in 1200, it too had to be captured by a royal army.

The resolution of one Norman dispute has affected the character of East Anglia ever since. Having moved his see from North Elmham to Thetford, Bishop Herfast, in about 1070, tried to establish himself at Bury St Edmunds. No doubt he hoped to become associated with the growing cult of St Edmund and the wealth of the Benedictine abbey there. However, Abbot Baldwin, by appealing to the Pope, visiting Rome and lobbying the king, successfully fought off the threat. So in 1094, the next bishop, Herbert de Losinga, moved his see to Norwich, where it has been ever since. Had Herfast succeeded, Bury would have had an abbey-cum-cathedral which would almost certainly have survived the Reformation.

In their simple strong style, the Normans rebuilt many parish churches founded in Anglo-Saxon times. Fritton and Wissington provide superb examples which have survived to this day. Unfortunately, the majority of these Norman structures were destroyed by later generations who extended, remodelled and rebuilt yet again. Even so, as Bob Carr's work at Ubbeston proved, Norman masonry does survive more often than guide books allow, but is disguised by the insertion of later doors and windows.

32 Framlingham Castle: rebuilt in 1189-1213 by Roger Bigod II, using the new fashion of curtain-wall with 13 flanking towers. In the foreground, earthworks of the Lower Court (left), contemporary with the walls, and the Bailey (right) of the first, Norman, castle.

33 *Westhall: Norman south door of the later 12th century. The Norman nave still survives as the south aisle of a later church. Traces of a Norman apsidal chancel can also be seen.*

34 *Wissett: one of the early round towers so characteristic of eastern Suffolk. It is probably late Anglo-Saxon in date. A blocked circular opening can be seen below the belfry window. Traces of the original wooden 'shuttering' have recently been recognised inside the windows.*

Monasticism (illus. 36)

35 *Moyse's Hall, Bury St Edmunds: a Norman house of the 12th century beside the Great Market.*

The Normans greatly stimulated the growth of religious orders and their 'houses'. Suffolk shared in this growth, though the early dominance of Bury abbey undoubtedly restricted the development of rival institutions. The main effect, therefore, was a considerable number of relatively small foundations, especially in the eastern half of the county. Most religious orders were represented. Benedictine monks were established in seven places other than Bury: the most important was Eye priory founded by Robert Malet, a few yards from his new castle. Benedictine nunneries were also built in the 12th century at Bungay and Redlingfield. Before 1155, the related Cluniacs had two small houses at Mendham and Wangford. The Cistercians had their only house at Sibton, founded in 1150 by William de Cayneto, and the Premonstratensians at Leiston, founded in 1183 by Sir Ranulph de Glanvill, justiciar of England.

By contrast, Augustinian canons were set up in no fewer than 13 places. Their establishments were mostly quite small, but there were two exceptions.

Ixworth was founded in 1170 by Gilbert Blunt, and grew into a community of about 20 canons. Butley was another foundation of Sir Ranulph de Glanvill, and was set up in the later 12th century. It had 36 canons by 1200, and was second only to Bury in its income. Of the various houses for women, the most important by far was Campsey Ash, for Augustinian canonesses. Founded *c*.1195 by Theobald de Valoines for 21 inmates, it attracted considerable endowments and became a fashionable resort for women of high birth.

All these institutions were overshadowed by the size and wealth of Bury abbey. At its greatest, it contained 80 Benedictine monks, a score of chaplains and over 100 retainers and servants. As well as being the centre of a major pilgrimage, it entertained kings and queens, housed parliaments, built up a famous manuscript library with over 2,000 volumes, and was said to be the scene of a preliminary meeting of barons which led to the granting of Magna Carta. Having acquired privileges and estates since Anglo-Saxon times, its annual income on the eve of the Dissolution was £1,656, over five times greater than that of its nearest rival in Suffolk.

36 *Medieval religious houses: the influence and prestige of Bury abbey clearly restricted the foundation of rival establishments in the west.*

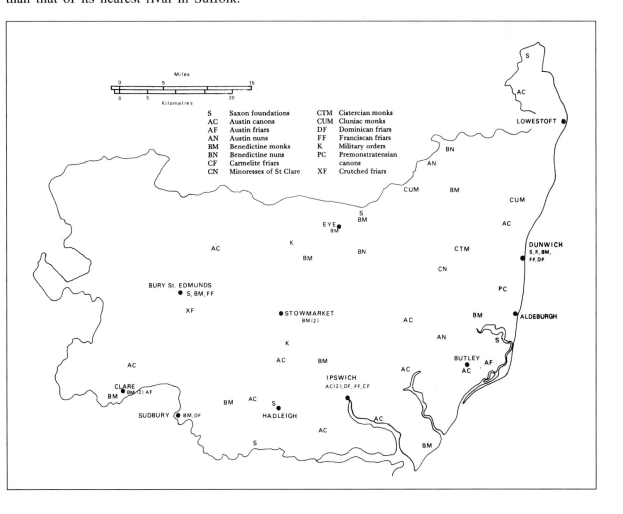

Miles

| 0 | 5 | 15 |

| 0 | 5 | 20 |

Kilometres

S	Saxon foundations	CTM	Cistercian monks
AC	Austin canons	CUM	Cluniac monks
AF	Austin friars	DF	Dominican friars
AN	Austin nuns	FF	Franciscan friars
BM	Benedictine monks	K	Military orders
BN	Benedictine nuns	PC	Premonstratensian
CF	Carmelite friars		canons
CN	Minoresses of St Clare	XF	Crutched friars

The abbey church itself was elaborately rebuilt after the Norman Conquest, beginning at the east end. By 1095 the choir had been finished, and the body of St Edmund was moved to a glittering new shrine behind the high altar (illus. 37; plate VI). The west end was not finally completed until the late 12th century. In its final form the abbey church was over 500 feet long with eastern apses, central tower, western tower and a west front nearly 250 feet across with triple porticos and flanking octagons—one of the greatest Romanesque churches in Europe. Over the same period a large number of conventual buildings was also erected, mainly on the north side of the great church, and the two parish churches of St Mary and St James were provided for the townsfolk. They all lay within a precinct wall which took in land that had formerly been part of the town. In the process an early north-south street running across the west end of the abbey church was diverted to the present line of Angel Hill, causing the right-angled bends which are still a feature of the town plan today. The main entrance of the abbey was the magnificent limestone gatehouse which is now known as the Norman Tower.

37 Bury abbey: the spiritual heart of East Anglia. At the east end of the huge Romanesque church, this crypt was excavated between 1957 and 1964. Above it, in mid-air, is the site of the high altar and the sacred shrine which contained the body of St Edmund.

Not only was Bury abbey splendidly rebuilt after the Norman Conquest, but the town too was greatly extended (illus. 38). Domesday Book tells us that Abbot Baldwin, between 1066 and 1086, allowed the building of 342 new houses on 'land which ... used to be ploughed and sown'. These houses were either in the immediate vicinity of the abbey, or more likely to its south around

the present St Mary's Square. Later, in the first half of the 12th century, the monastic precinct was extended to its final form with perimeter wall, Norman tower and parish churches. At least two earlier north-south roads were severed or diverted by this development. Immediately outside the precinct and on the western slope of the Lark valley, a remarkable grid of streets was then laid out, all parallel or at right angles, constituting one of the best examples in Britain of deliberate urban planning. This new 12th-century quarter of the town included a major new market place, a huge rectangle measuring 200 by 100 yards, which still exists but is two-thirds built over. Finally, the whole Anglo-Saxon and Norman town, sprawling down the valley, was enclosed by a long curving rampart broken by five gates.

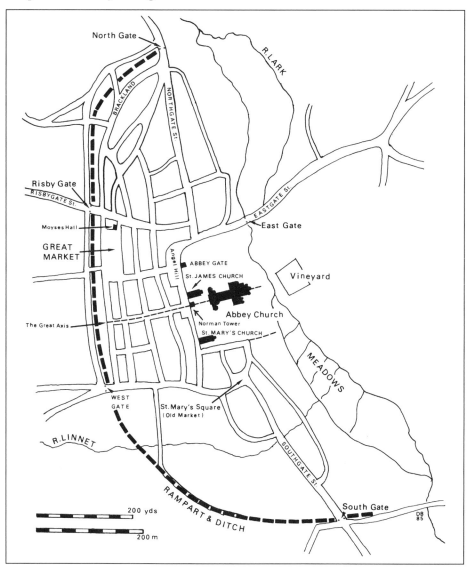

38 *Medieval Bury St Edmunds: the planned grid of streets, laid out probably in the early 12th century, hinges on the great axis of Churchgate Street, the abbey church and St Edmund's shrine. The westward expansion of the monastic precinct broke the line of an early north-south road.*

39 *Small bronze-gilt figure of St John grieving, c.1180, ploughed up at Rattlesden. Less than four inches high.*

One of Suffolk's outstanding historical documents is the Chronicle of Jocelin of Brakelond. Jocelin was a monk of Bury who eventually became cellarer of the abbey. His chronicle is a biography of Abbot Samson, a strong administrator and disciplinarian who ruled the abbey from 1182 to 1211. Although it is written in a tone of admiration, it subtly hints at the abbot's faults as well—for example his frequent high-handedness and insensitivity. 'No one', wrote H.E. Butler, a modern editor, 'has given us such an intensely vivid picture of the life of a great monastery.' For example, the election of Samson in the presence of Richard I at Waltham is brilliantly described and, subsequently, his walking barefoot into the abbey to prostrate himself before the high altar and then to kiss the shrine of St Edmund.

Manorial Society in the High Middle Ages

In the 13th century Suffolk reached the height of its early importance and prosperity. It had, by medieval standards, a dense and growing population which exerted great pressure on the land and also gave, for some at least, new economic opportunities. Landlords and major tenants responded to the increased demand for food and to rising agricultural prices by improving the productivity of their farming and making determined use of all kinds of land. Those with little or no land had a choice of picking up full-time or part-time employment in various expanding forms of domestic industry, crafts or retailing. A good example is the increasing reliance of the poor on the brewing and selling of ale, which became a major cottage industry. In the last resort those who were unable to make ends meet in the countryside could migrate to major towns like Ipswich, Norwich or Bury, or to the market centres which were springing up more frequently in East Anglia than in any other part of Britain.

Some impression of manorial life in Suffolk can be gleaned from courtrolls, accounts and surveys. In each manor the lord had his 'Hall' or courthouse which was the administrative heart of the community—regardless of whether he actually lived there or not. He, or his bailiff, cultivated a substantial home farm (the 'demesne') which was partly around the Hall in the form of hedged fields and partly scattered and intermixed with the lands of tenants. In the later 13th century, these demesnes reached their maximum size, as the lords tried to increase their incomes from direct farming. Many lords also owned watermills, windmills, the right of presenting the parson to the church, and various judicial privileges such as the right of having stocks, pillories and even gallows. By this period, manors were by no means equivalent to parishes, and had often been subdivided by a process known as subinfeudation. At Risby, for example, three manor houses were virtually contiguous—the original capital manor of Risby and two others called Charmans and Quyes.

By about 1300 the inhabitants of Suffolk had almost doubled their numbers, from about 72,000 at the time of the Norman Conquest to about 140,000. Calculations can be made, at a local level, on the basis of archaeological evidence, or from manorial and fiscal documents. Thus, the 13th-century parish of Mendlesham contained not only the main village and market, but another hamlet around a green and no fewer than 90 scattered farmhouses—a far higher

40 *Little Wenham Hall: a fortified brick house of c.1270-80.*

number than at any period before or since. At Lidgate in *c*.1066 the population
was about 170; by the early 14th century there were over 350 inhabitants. (Even
in the first census of 1801, Lidgate's population was only 323 and had apparently not recovered to its level before the Black Death.) The number of sons
a man left behind at his death could also indicate what was happening to the
population as a whole. In 1257-60, 10 men of Hinderclay were succeeded by
17 sons—a high rate which, after 1300, was to fall drastically.

41 *St Stephen's chapel,
Bures: an isolated chapel
of early 13th-century
date.*

Under such pressure, land was used intensively and with great ecological
sensitivity. The arable acreage, much of it in the form of open-fields, was at its
maximum, but at the same time complementary forms of land use were greatly
prized—pasture, hay-meadows, marshes, fens or turbaries, commons, woods
and under-woods. The market in land was vigorous, and the average holding
and the average plot were extremely small. Richard Smith has calculated that
in 13th-century Redgrave, 26 per cent of the holdings were less than one acre,
and that the average plot of land mentioned in transactions was about half an
acre. At Semer in 1230, an inheritance in an open field was divided among five
brothers: each of them received 'a quarter of three parts of half an acre divided
into five'. Furthermore, the basic farming units called 'tenements' or 'full
lands', whose origins go back at least to the 12th century, were by this time
highly fragmented. In 1289, Ralph Mercator of Redgrave farmed seven acres
and one rood, but they lay in 13 different tenements; the largest piece of land
within his holding was 5½ roods (just over 1¼ acres). His brother Walter had
a holding with exactly the same size and distribution—the classic effect of
partible inheritance. But although forms of inheritance could be important, their
effects could always be offset by personal arrangements and transactions. It was
the basic pressure of population, of mouths to feed, that ensured that the land
was intensively farmed, highly fragmented and intermixed, especially in the
large arable open-fields.

In return for their land, peasants were expected to do labour services for
their lords or give money in lieu. A survey of the manor of Melford as late as
1386, specifies nearly 9,000 labour services for which villeins were responsible
mainly in the autumn and winter months. At Rattlesden in 1251 a villein with
about 20 acres of land had the following annual obligations to his lord the
Bishop of Ely: he had to pay 29½d. for various dues, to give three hens at
Christmas and 20 eggs at Easter, and to do two 'works' each week from
October to August. Extra works could be demanded by the lord if he needed
them. His actual duties included ploughing, seeding and harrowing, scattering
manure, weeding, mowing the lord's meadow, scattering, binding, cocking and
carrying hay, taking a cart of hay to Hitcham, reaping in autumn, binding and
carrying sheaves, threshing and carrying grain, beans and peas, making malt,
digging and cleaning ditches, cutting and carrying underwood, making hurdles,
hedging and thatching. In addition he had to provide a horse and cart for
various journeys, including two a year to Ipswich and two a year to Ely. He had
to take his corn to the lord's mill and could not sell his foals or oxen without
the lord's permission. Nor could his sheep lie in the lord's fold. He had to be
prepared to pay 'gersum' on the marriage of his daughter, 'childwyte' if his

42 *Rumburgh church, originally a small Benedictine priory: tower of 13th century, the same width as the nave.*

daughter had an illegitimate child, and a personal tax called 'tallage'. On his death, a 'heriot' consisting of his best beast or 22d. was payable, and his wife 'shall immediately begin to work'. At East Bergholt, the indignity of being an unfree tenant, liable to pay a heriot, was further underlined by his having to fix on his house a special sign called 'Le cople', while every person subject to the jurisdiction of the local leet court had to put a cross on the front of his house.

One very unusual glimpse of ordinary villagers is afforded by the detailed returns for the Lay Subsidy of 1283 which survive, out of the whole of England, only for the Hundred of Blackbourn in north Suffolk. They list the crops grown and stock kept by the people of each parish. The large parish of Bardwell (3,142 acres) had 128 taxpayers ranging from the lord William de Pakenham who paid 17s. 10½d., to Botilda de Brakelond who paid only 3d. Here, on the edge of the sandy Breckland, barley was easily the most important grain grown, followed by rye; more peas and beans were grown than wheat and oats. With its wide heaths, Bardwell had 1,313 sheep, but it also had plenty of other animals—587 pigs, 456 cattle and 89 horses. The lord, of course, owned most of the animals, including the only bull and the one boar. A fairly prosperous 'peasant' like Richard Hail grew four kinds of cereal, plus peas and beans, and owned two horses, five cattle and 11 sheep, whereas a poorer man like Thomas Biscop grew only barley and had one cow, two pigs and five sheep.

At Walsham-le-Willows, a parish of 2,760 acres on heavier land in the east of Blackbourn Hundred, the balance of farming was significantly different. Again, barley was the most important crop, but was followed by peas and oats; wheat, rye and beans were relatively unimportant. Only in the growing of peas did Walsham actually outstrip Bardwell. As for animals, sheep and pigs were much less numerous, while horses and cattle were relatively more important. Manorial accounts suggest that in High Suffolk wheat was the dominant grain, while in major valleys like the Waveney dairying and cheese-production were already economic specialisations.

Contrary to the persistent myth that villagers stayed put all their lives, there is now abundant evidence to show that quite ordinary people, even in the Middle Ages, often moved house over short distances, up to 30 miles, and sometimes much further. For the period after 1300, John Ridgard has found that at Flixton near Bungay, 55 per cent of the personal names of the manor disappeared every five years. Some people may simply have changed their names, while other families undoubtedly survived through a female line. Nevertheless, a substantial proportion must have left the manor. Similarly, the Lay Subsidy of 1327 contains many surnames which imply that people had not been born in the place where they were living. In the village of Mutford near Lowestoft, the lord's family came from Hengrave near Bury, and other families derived from Gapton near Yarmouth, Blofield near Norwich and Feltwell in west Norfolk. The trend is even more obvious among the inhabitants of towns. Ipswich, for instance had attracted many families from eastern Suffolk, from places like Holbrook, Creeting, Akenham and Hoo, and others from further afield from places like Preston near Lavenham, Hoxne in the Waveney valley, Wimbush in Essex and Castle Acre in west Norfolk.

Another type of surname reveals where people actually lived within their parish. At Stanton in the 13th century families named 'del Char' and 'de Dale' clearly lived at the hamlet now called Stanton Chair (meaning the place where the river took a sharp turn) and where the two Dale Farms are today. At Wetherden, William de Dersham lived where Dersham Farm is today while Henry Motoun was almost certainly his neighbour at Mutton Hall.

Markets, fairs and towns

The early Middle Ages saw a rapid expansion in various forms of industry and commerce, and the consequent foundation of scores of local markets. This 'Commercial Revolution' was not entirely new as urban life had undoubtedly developed significantly in the later Saxon period. At the time of the Norman Conquest, Domesday Book recorded nine market towns in Suffolk, and undoubtedly omitted others. A few more appeared in the next century, as at Eye where William Malet encouraged a market outside his new castle, and at the port and planned town of Orford where a large rectangular market place was laid out between castle and church. However, the main expansion came after 1200. Norman Scarfe calculates that no fewer than 70 markets appeared in

43 Needham Market: a town created by the Bishop of Ely along a major road in one corner of his manor of Barking. Market charter of 1226. The chapel existed by 1251, was rebuilt 1480-1500, and did not become a parish church until 1901. For centuries the dead were carried along the Carnser for burial at the mother church of Barking. Based on Pennington's map of 1772.

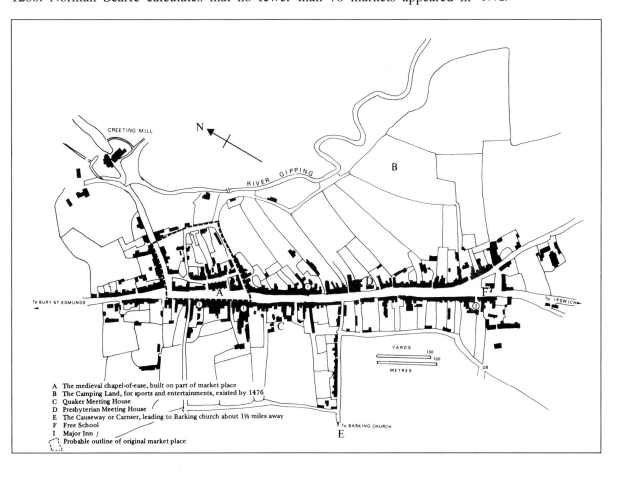

A The medieval chapel-of-ease, built on part of market place
B The Camping Land, for sports and entertainments, existed by 1476
C Quaker Meeting House
D Presbyterian Meeting House
E The Causeway or Carnser, leading to Barking church about 1½ miles away
F Free School
I Major Inn
⌐ Probable outline of original market place

44 *Thornham Parva: painted figure of St Edmund on altarpiece of c.1300.*

Suffolk between 1227 and 1310, and that by the end of the Middle Ages the total was around a hundred. Very few markets were created after 1350, the most important being Aldeburgh in 1547. In most cases a weekly market was officially created by the grant of a royal charter, and was accompanied by an annual fair lasting two days or more. Thus, the Earl of Oxford received a charter in 1257 for his manor of Lavenham, giving him a market on Tuesdays and a Whitsuntide fair lasting three days. Aspall near Debenham is one of the two places in England where Domesday Book mentions a fair—though others must have existed, even then.

Medieval markets were thick on the ground, especially in the eastern half of Suffolk. In a block of country no more than six miles across, a Norman market existed at Kelsale, 13th-century markets at Middleton, Sizewell and Saxmundham, and 14th-century markets at Aldringham and Leiston. A seventh market was mentioned at Knodishall in the early 17th century. In fact, markets were often much closer than the six-and-two-thirds miles recommended by the 13th-century lawyer, Henry Bracton. Around Bury St Edmunds, however, there was a conspicuous lack of markets for a radius of about eight miles, the nearest competitors being Barrow and Ixworth.

The actual sites chosen for markets varied greatly. In most cases, landlords speculated by trying to upgrade and expand existing villages. Thus, at Mildenhall and Saxmundham, it is possible to identify an early agricultural community associated with church and manor-house, and a later urban extension around an open space suitable for marketing. Sometimes advantage was taken of a major bridging point, as at Bungay or Bures, or even of a ferry as at Brandon. In a few cases, a virgin site was chosen to take advantage of a major road. Thus Newmarket grew up at the southern end of Exning manor, to exploit a sheltered hollow along the Icknield Way. Similarly, Botesdale grew up in a corner of Redgrave, and Needham in a corner of Barking, both to exploit major through-roads (illus. 43).

Most markets probably had an unofficial or experimental existence before their owners obtained legal charters while the markets of Haverhill, Lidgate, Boxford and East Bergholt never did get official recognition. It is also important to remember that all these medieval markets were not co-existent. Not only were they founded over several centuries, but some never got beyond the planning stage, some failed early and others merely functioned at a low level. For example, it does not seem that the 13th-century charters for Felsham and Wissett led to any significant developments, in building or in commerce.

45 *The Great Gate of Bury Abbey, rebuilt after the uprising of the town in 1327.*

4

Crisis and Revival, 1300-1530

During this period, England underwent a series of profound changes, socially, economically and psychologically. Suffolk, being part of a populous and economically advanced region, illustrated these trends very clearly—in its manorial administration, agricultural practices, industrial development, social structure and even in its religious thinking. The new world which emerged in the 15th century was, however, born of several severe crises which rocked society to its roots.

46 *Medieval seal of borough of Dunwich, once a great port.*

Social unrest at the beginning of the 14th century was especially apparent among the townsmen of Bury St Edmunds. In 1305 they made one of their periodic attempts to win independence from the abbey, earning themselves a suspended fine of £333 and 50 barrels of wine. In England as a whole, disastrous harvests in 1315 and 1316 were succeeded by the spread of cattle disease and, in the 1320s, by years of drought. These economic disruptions stimulated new unrest which eventually led to the deposition and death of Edward II in 1327. In that year the burgesses of Bury launched the bloodiest of all their uprisings against the abbey.

In the September of 1326, Edward II's queen, Isabella, together with the young Prince Edward and supporters from France, landed at Walton near Felixstowe and pursued the king's forces across England. Such a situation presented an ideal opportunity for insurrection and, in the following January, just before the king's deposition was announced, crowds organised by the burgesses pillaged Bury abbey. Several months later, the rebels were finally subdued and 30 cartloads of prisoners were sent off to Norwich. A number of lives had been lost, the gateway into the great court had been destroyed and many internal buildings burned, among them Bradfield Hall (which has often been confused with the village of Bradfield Combust). On the other hand, little permanent benefit seems to have been gained by the burgesses, many of whom lost their heads and others their possessions.

The Black Death

It was not social unrest, however, which had the greatest effect on East Anglian life in the 14th century, but the movements of the common flea which carried the dreaded infection known as the Black Death. Introduced into England from the Mediterranean in the summer of 1348, the plague reached its peak in Suffolk in the summer of the next year. Within a few months, between a third and a half of the population was mown down. Numerous deaths among villein

47 *Burgate church: large brass of Sir William de Burgate (died 1409) and wife.*

48 *Wenhaston: the rare survival of a medieval 'doom' painting, on boards which formerly filled the chancel arch. Christ in Majesty presides over the weighing of souls: some are sent to Hell (right) and others to Paradise (left). The unpainted sections show where the rood or cross stood, and the figures of SS Mary and John.*

tenants were reported to manorial courts. At Walsham-le-Willows, 102 deaths were listed in June 1349, while at Redgrave the total reached 169 in July. The normal number of deaths in these manors, during these months, would have been less than ten. Two-thirds of the benefices in Norwich diocese (which then included Suffolk) are estimated to have been made vacant, for priests who visited the sick and buried the dead were especially vulnerable.

A great deal of myth has unfortunately grown up around the Black Death. It was no doubt catastrophic, but it was not solely responsible for some of the results frequently attributed to it, such as the shifting of villages and the isolation of churches. In fact, the rural population was shrinking already, well before the coming of the Black Death. Professor Thrupp has shown that the 'replacement rate' at which sons succeeded fathers was falling steadily on certain East Anglian manors throughout the first half of the 14th century. In the case of Hinderclay, the replacement rate fell by over 40 per cent before 1349. Another sign of dwindling population is the untilled ground recorded in 1341 by the Inquisition of the Ninths. Nearly 1,700 acres, in eight parishes of Risbridge Hundred, were reported as abandoned. The Black Death did, of course, accelerate these downward trends but was not their sole cause.

Although the passing of the epidemic left many vacant holdings, there is no evidence to support the belief, so beloved of local historians, that villages were frequently and immediately deserted. Where field-walking as been carried out extensively, as at Mendlesham and Walsham, scores of abandoned sites have been discovered, but they were usually abandoned before the Black Death or well after. Isolated churches, which are a major feature of the East Anglian landscape, are often mistakenly designated 'plague churches', yet the villages which were once associated with them migrated long before 1349. The only likely example of a village 'killed by the Black Death' is Alston or Alteston. It had been functioning as an autonomous parish in 1341 when its parishioners paid significant tithes and altar-dues, but by 1362 was united ecclesiastically with its neighbour Trimley St Martin.

Although the Black Death reduced population by at least a third, the homes of dead tenants were usually claimed by a legitimate heir and not immediately left to rot. It was the frequent recurrence of plague in the later 14th and 15th centuries which was responsible for many vacant holdings and shrunken villages. At Norton, for instance, the court rolls record the neglect and decay of properties

49 *Little Livermere: a deserted village photographed in 1960, before it was ploughed. Notice the streets, house-platforms, property boundaries and roofless church. A single farm now occupies the site.*

throughout the 15th century, while a survey of Walsham-le-Willows in 1581 mentions a number of former tenements and messuages which had probably been abandoned in the same period.

As some farmsteads and holdings were being deserted, lords of manors were leasing out increasing amounts of demesne land as a means of raising ready cash. The combined effect was to give those farmers who remained the welcome opportunity of substantially enlarging their holdings. Seventy-four parishes scattered around Suffolk, which were listed in 1428 as each having fewer than 50 inhabitants, had by 1524 a high average of 115 acres to each household. At Redgrave account rolls show the leasing of demesne rising from 42 cases in 1371 to 98 in 1391 and 123 in 1421, while surveys of a few years later record holdings enlarged with portions of abandoned tenements. In this evidence the origins of the East Anglian yeoman farmer can be discerned, so important a figure in the rural community throughout later centuries.

With the increasing acreage of holdings came an awareness of the value of consolidating and enclosing land, especially in clay-covered High Suffolk. Much indisputable evidence of early enclosure is found, making nonsense of the oft-repeated statement that it was only from the 18th century that fields were defined by hedges and ditches. 'Closes' are frequently mentioned in medieval wills, while court rolls often show the lords, lessees and tenants of High Suffolk enclosing their land on a piecemeal basis from the second half of the 14th century onwards. Between 1422 and 1501 Littlehaugh Manor at Norton witnessed 190 cases of enclosure and encroachment, with the greatest frequency in the 1430s and '40s. By Elizabethan times, enclosure was well advanced, as

50 *Sir Adam Bacon, fully vested priest with alb, stole, maniple and chasuble c.1320: brass in Oulton church drawn by J.S. Cotman, now lost.*

51 *Rougham: a mature, curving hedge containing a rich mixture of native species. This feature, with its accompanying ditch, probably resulted from the late medieval enclosure of open-fields, and is therefore at least 500 years old. As worthy a monument as a timber-framed farmhouse of the same period.*

many surveys and maps show. Furthermore, the resulting fields of Suffolk were often in the form of grassland, either permanently or in rotation, and they held cows more often than the notorious sheep which 'ate up men'. By 1577, 75 per cent of Walsham was enclosed and 85 per cent under grass. Areas like that around Debenham were supporting, by the mid-16th century at least, fairly large herds of dairy cattle and producing quantities of cheese.

The Peasants' Revolt

Despite these new trends, or perhaps because of them, major unrest broke out again in 1381 in the form of the Peasants' Revolt. This movement against the ruling classes was supported by a large cross-section of the community, though unfree villeins were greatly in the majority. A combination of irritants, some the aftermath of the Black Death, exacerbated by high taxes and controls on wages, and whipped up by eloquent members of the minor clergy, provoked considerable violence and bloodshed. Suffolk names feature prominently among the *dramatis personae* of the event. The Archbishop of Canterbury, surnamed Sudbury after his birthplace, was the son of a wealthy local merchant; he was slain by a London mob on Tower Hill. One of our most extraordinary (and grisly) relics is his pickled head preserved at St Gregory's church in his native town. Chief justice John de Cavendish was one of the first targets of the Suffolk mob, who relieved him of his goods and head. On the rebel side, John Wrawe, chaplain of Sudbury and the Suffolk counterpart of Jack Straw, terrorised the area around Bury St Edmunds and claimed to have the support of notable county families such as the Tollemaches, Bedingfields and Woolverstones. All was over, though, in a fortnight. A leading part in the armed suppression of the revolt was played by Henry Despenser, bishop of Norwich.

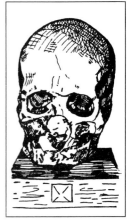

52 *St Gregory's, Sudbury: preserved head of Archbishop Simon, murdered during Peasants' Revolt.*

The prime aim of the rebels was to break the hold of the lords over their villein tenants; hence the frequent pillaging of manor houses and 'burning of the rolls' in an attempt to eradicate evidence of villein status. While the inevitable consequence of the rising was military and judicial suppression, and Parliament was quick to emphasise the continuance of villein status, yet the hold of lords over their tenants, already eroded before 1381, continued steadily to weaken. By the middle of the 15th century, Suffolk's manorial documents show few references to labour services, which were the most severe of the villeins' traditional burdens. Grants of manumission (the releasing of bondmen from servitude) often occur early in that century and some wills, such as that of Sir Andrew Boteler of Great Waldingfield in 1430, leave instructions for all bondmen on specific manors to be given their freedom. On the other hand under the most conservative lords, like the Dukes of Norfolk, villein status was strictly maintained well into Elizabethan times.

Industrial growth

While those (still probably the majority of Suffolk's population) whose livelihood lay solely in agriculture enjoyed an improved standard of living in the later 14th and 15th centuries, the leaders of commerce and industry had a genuine chance of becoming rich. In the period from approximately 1450 to

53 *Seal of Suffolk's aulnager, royal official who inspected cloth.*

54 *Deanery Tower, Hadleigh, built when Archdeacon Pykenham was rector, c.1470-97.*

55 *Success symbolised in stone: the base of Lavenham's tower, begun c.1486, bears the merchant mark of Thomas Spring II; the top, finished c.1525, displays the heraldic shield of Thomas Spring III 'the great clothier'.*

1530 the cloth industry reached a major peak of prosperity, and especially so in the main broadcloth area of south Suffolk—roughly a triangle with points at Clare, Bury St Edmunds and East Bergholt.

The evidence of craft-surnames and the occurrence of fulling mills in the 13th and 14th centuries at Hadleigh, Sudbury and Bury St Edmunds show that the Suffolk broadcloth industry was in existence, albeit on a small scale, well before the supposed arrival of Flemish weavers in the 1330s. Although the Flemings helped, no doubt, to reinvigorate the industry over the country as a whole, their settlement in East Anglia seems to have been confined to Norwich and Colchester, and no foreign influence is discernible at all in Suffolk at that period. Indeed, when lists of resident aliens do become available for the following century, the few foreigners involved in the production of cloth prove to have been Italians.

The production of broadcloth, chiefly in the Hundreds of Babergh and Cosford, increased dramatically in the 15th century. The industry gave employment to large numbers of men, women and children in the different processes of spinning, weaving, dyeing, fulling and shearing, but the wealthiest group were the clothiers or clothmakers. They were the capitalists of the system, buying the wool, organising its processing and marketing the finished product. Wills proved during the late 15th and early 16th centuries in the highest probate court of the country (the Prerogative Court of Canterbury) indicate the rising number of these entrepreneurs and where they lived. Lavenham had the most clothiers while Boxford, Long Melford, Hadleigh, Nayland, Waldingfield and East Bergholt followed closely behind. The relative wealth of individuals can be seen in the subsidy returns of 1524. Alice Spring, widow of Thomas Spring III, the 'Rich Clothier' of Lavenham, was worth a mammoth £1,000 in possessions, second highest in the county to the Duke of Norfolk. Her husband, in his day, had been the wealthiest man in England outside the nobility, owning at the time of his death 26 manors and property in 76 other places. Similarly, nearly half of all those assessed at £200 or more in 1524 prove to have been clothiers.

The relative importance of cloth-producing towns in the 15th century can be gauged from the returns of a tax official called the aulnager. The annual totals of cloths produced, as distinct from the number of clothiers at work, show that the greatest output came from Hadleigh, followed by Lavenham, Bury St Edmunds, Ipswich, Nayland, Waldingfield, Long Melford and Sudbury. In several cases it has to be assumed that cloth-producing villages in their vicinity were also included.

A muster roll of 1522, surviving for the Hundred of Babergh only, indicates the number of clothworkers in each parish. Boxford had the largest total (60), mainly weavers, whereas Lavenham (34), Glemsford (20) and Nayland (14) had the greatest number of clothiers. Long Melford, on the other hand had more fullers than anywhere else, and Nayland more shearmen. These figures show that parishes tended to have individual specialisations, but were also linked and dependent on each other.

Kersey and Lindsey, two places traditionally associated with clothmaking, do not feature in any official lists, although they may well be included under

Hadleigh. Considerable doubt exists, however, as to whether they really gave their names to kinds of cloth. 'Kerseys' or 'Carseys' (probably derived from an early Arabic word) were narrow cloths produced in several parts of England, while 'Linsey' implies linen, as in linsey-wolsey which was a mixture of linen and wool.

56 Norton: carving on a 15th-century misericord which depicts a lady preparing wool for spinning. She is using a pair of 'cards' which resemble wire-brushes.

The architectural legacy

The evidence remaining today for all this late-medieval wealth is largely in the form of buildings—fine timber-framed houses and Perpendicular churches. Although 'the great rebuilding' is a phrase originally coined for the period 1570-1640, it might equally well be applied here. Individuals extended, adapted and rebuilt their houses while parishes did the same with their churches. One can virtually judge the wealth of a place in the 15th century by the amount of building done, or not done, on its church. Thus, at Lavenham and Long Melford, the churches were mainly rebuilt, yet on the Breckland the average church may have had the occasional new window or door but retained much more of its fabric from earlier centuries.

Architecture is, of course, subject to changes of fashion and technology. During the first half of the 14th century the Decorated style was in vogue. In churches new windows with 'curvilinear' tracery and ogee arches were then replacing Early English lancets and Norman splayed openings. From this period we have many fine east windows as at Mildenhall and Monk Soham, and more spacious chancels like Brandon and Raydon with their attractive spirelets. Fortunately, these did *not* get rebuilt in the 15th century.

From about 1360 onwards, the Perpendicular style came into fashion producing in many parishes the 'typical Suffolk church'. Varying amounts of building were undertaken but the great majority of parishes managed at least to introduce

57 The mythical sciapod who sheltered beneath his giant foot: bench-end at Dennington.

58 *Walberswick: a magnificent 15th-century church which, because of the port's economic decline and depopulation, became ruinous. In 1695 the church was largely dismantled and only part of the south aisle retained for worship. For building the tower, the original contract of 1426 survives.*

some up-to-date windows. Large numbers of towers went up, and many fine aisles, chapels and porches. Parishes tried to keep up with their neighbours and paid them the compliment of copying certain features. This is seen in the building instructions given to masons: Halesworth and Tunstall towers were copied at Walberswick, while Framsden and Brandeston were the patterns for Helmingham. Soon, hardly a church remained that had not organised some improvement to its fabric.

Internal features, too, were the subject of great care and expense. During this period most parishes seem to have rebuilt their rood screens and lofts, put in fine carved benches and raised beautifully carved roofs. They frequently installed new fonts, especially those depicting the seven sacraments, Easter sepulchres and tabernacles to house statues. Even where these features survive, the brilliant colours with which they were decorated have largely gone. It is, therefore, only by reading documents and using the imagination that the full magnificence of these church interiors before the Reformation can be reconstructed.

Much of this work on churches was financed by individuals, chiefly for 'the good of their souls'. Such beneficence was sometimes recorded by inscriptions in the stonework, outstandingly so at Long Melford and Stratford St Mary, or by inscriptions in less durable glass but fortunately recorded by early antiquaries, as at Parham. The majority, though, merely made entries in the backs of their service books or on their bede rolls, and these have long since vanished, leaving us to piece together what we can from surviving wills. These record the gifts of what an Elizabethan parish clerk of Eye termed 'the frank and devowte hartes of the people' as, for instance, to the tower of Eye itself from 1453 to 1479; to the south porch at Boxford from 1441 to 1480; to the chancel of Blythburgh from 1443 to 1475; and many others. It has been calculated that Lavenham church, between 1485 and 1540, received gifts and bequests totalling £2,287, a prodigious sum when a labourer's daily wage hovered between 4d. and 6d.

59 *Cratfield: 15th-century font depicting the Seven Sacraments.*

In Lavenham's case, 70 per cent of the donors were involved in the cloth trade, and it is in clothmaking areas, as would be expected, that some of the finest churches are to be found. (While they can, with some justice, be called 'cloth churches', they should never be referred to as 'wool churches' because most of the wool certainly was not grown locally.) Commerce of a more general kind, and of course agriculture, also generated prosperity and this accounts for such fine churches as Mildenhall and St Mary's, Bury St Edmunds. Down the coast, a string of magnificent 15th-century churches was built from the proceeds of trade and fishing: Lowestoft, Kessingland, Covehithe, Southwold, Walberswick, Blythburgh and Aldeburgh. Fishing, before its decline in the 16th and 17th centuries, provided an extra bonus as can be seen in the churchwardens' accounts for Walberswick. A share of the catch, known as the town dole, was traditionally paid to the parish to repair the quay, but it was frequently diverted towards the repair and rebuilding of the church.

Another source of wealth was warfare. John Leland found that the fortunes of wealthy English families of the 16th century were not infrequently founded on the battlefields of France a century earlier. In East Anglia, too, wealth could be based on plunder and ransom money, which could subsequently benefit local churches. Fine work at Wingfield church was paid for by the de la Poles; they were originally wool merchants from Hull who for several generations supplied the Crown with money and arms. The colourful chantry chapel in Dennington church commemorates Lord Bardolph who distinguished himself at Agincourt, while the tower and aisles at Westhorpe, begun long before, were completed after 1419 with money accumulated by Sir William de Elmham, a member of Richard II's court. An even more remarkable instance was the total rebuilding, just before 1400, of Stowlangtoft church by Robert Ashfield, a former servant of the Black Prince.

60 *Brass of Thomas Powlner, rich merchant of Ipswich, who died 1525. Now in Christchurch Mansion.*

When a church was rebuilt, not only had the money to be found but the whole project planned and organised. The churchwardens and leading members of the community would normally have seen to this, but in at least two instances 'project directors' were clearly at work. Testators at Lavenham refer to promises made to 'my lord of Oxenford' (John de Vere, 13th Earl of Oxford), while those of Long Melford left money to be spent 'at the discretion of Master John Clopton'. It is no doubt due to these two influential patrons that Lavenham and Melford possess two of the finest parish churches in England.

61 *Leiston Abbey, founded 1182 and rebuilt in the late 14th century: the Premonstratensian church, looking west. After the Dissolution, the ruinous abbey became a farmstead. Until the early 20th century, the roofed section on the right was used as a barn.*

62 *Lavenham church which, apart from the chancel, was magnificently rebuilt from 1485 to 1525. Money-raising was encouraged by the lord of the manor, 13th Earl of Oxford. Fifty donors, of whom 35 were connected with the cloth industry, left £2,287 in their wills. Over £1,000 of that total came from the estate of Thomas Spring III, whose chantry lies south of the chancel.*

Surprisingly, much of the extensive refurbishing of churches took place during the Wars of the Roses. Wealthy landowners might well have been putting money into church-building on the one hand, yet financing a military expedition on the other. In the final battle at Bosworth Field in 1485, Suffolk was well represented. The Duke of Norfolk, who as Sir John Howard had contributed to the new tower at Stoke by Nayland, commanded the vanguard of Richard III's army, many of them recruited from Howard manors in Suffolk. Opposing him in the centre of Henry of Richmond's army was the 13th Earl of Oxford, Lavenham's benefactor. Nearby, William Brandon of Henham, whose father had recently contributed to Wangford's new aisle, was Henry's standard-bearer. In the course of the battle the Duke of Norfolk lost his life while attempting to break through the Earl of Oxford's ranks, while Brandon was transfixed by Richard's lance in the king's final great charge. De Vere, the only survivor of the three, was rewarded by the victorious Henry VII with many lucrative offices.

63 *Fressingfield: the* Fox and Goose, *formerly the guildhall, built c.1502 on the edge of the churchyard to remove sacrilegious drinking from the church.*

5

Reformation and Division, 1530-1630

Long before the 16th century, demands for religious reform had come from Lollards, followers of John Wycliffe who died in 1384. William White and Hugh Pie, who had operated Lollard schools in the Waveney valley, were executed in 1428, and a spate of trials took place in Norwich in the three following years. Many of the accused, the majority of whom came from the area around Beccles and Bungay, were vehemently opposed to such religious practices as praying to saints, the use of images and pilgrimages, oral confession and the belief in transubstantiation. Those found guilty were sentenced to flogging and had to do penance in their parish churches and graveyards.

64 *East Bergholt church: the west tower left unfinished when parishioners ran out of motivation and money at the time of the Reformation.*

After this period of persecution, little is heard of Lollard teaching but, almost exactly a century later, similar views were being voiced by the followers of Luther. One of the most important was Thomas Bilney, a Norfolk-born priest who spent some 18 months preaching in East Anglia before his arrest in 1527. His visit to Hadleigh, where he inveighed against pilgrimages and the worship of saints and relics, seems to have been particularly effective. Among his many converts were Guy Glazen, shoemaker of Eye, later punished for uttering obscenities against the cross at Eye Priory, and Thomas Rose, the Hadleigh curate, whose preaching led a gang of men to burn the Holy Rood of Dovercourt. Another Suffolk reformer was John Bale, a native of Covehithe but better known as a playwright and Bishop of Ossory in Ireland, who in 1536 was accused of inflammatory preaching at Thorndon where he was curate.

The majority of Suffolk's inhabitants, on the other hand, were far more conservative. Judging by their wills, almost all the laity and most of the clergy continued, until the death of Henry VIII, to provide for their souls and invoke the prayers of saints. Nevertheless, Suffolk folk cannot have been unaware of the national decisions which were beginning to affect their localities, and their gifts to the fabric of parish churches decreased significantly.

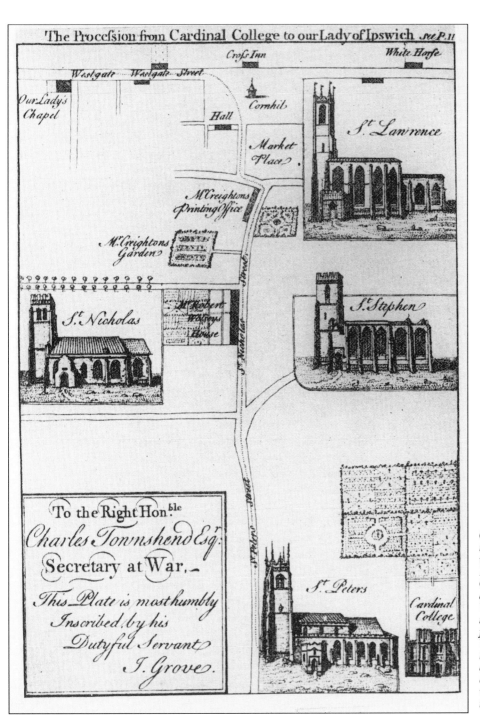

The Procession from Cardinal College to our Lady of Ipswich *see P.11*

65 *Two vanished institutions of medieval Ipswich: J. Grove's map of 1761 shows Our Lady's Chapel which contained a famous image of the Virgin Mary, and Cardinal College which was founded by Thomas Wolsey, built 1528-9, and largely demolished a year or two later. Had the college survived, Ipswich would be very different today.*

66 *Gedding Hall: gatehouse of c.1530 with moat.*

A new religious order

The first of these changes came in 1534. The Pope was replaced by Henry as Head of the English church and 'Peter's Pence', the traditional payment to Rome, was no longer demanded of each parish. In 1536, holy days (that is, holidays when no work was expected) were reduced from about 90 a year to under thirty. Under the 'Act for the dissolution of the lesser monasteries' of 1536, the first of the religious houses, the Cistercian abbey of Sibton and the nunneries of Bungay and Campsey, were closed and their property confiscated by the Crown. (Five small priories had, in fact, been closed in the previous decade by that most successful native of Ipswich, Cardinal Wolsey, in order to endow his college and school in the town.) The remaining 28 houses of Suffolk succumbed by 1540. Of these only Bury St Edmunds was powerful and rich enough to be dealt with under the subsequent Act of 1539, relating to the dissolution of the 'greater monasteries'.

It was at this time also that changes were first seen in the fabric and furnishing of parish churches. The royal injunctions of 1538, reflecting the preaching of reformers against saints and images, forbade the placing of candles before images and other 'superstitious practices', and no doubt encouraged the destruction that year of the famous images of Our Lady at Walsingham and Ipswich. All mention of Thomas à Becket, an archbishop who had dared to defy a king, was ordered to be removed from churches. This caused Mildenhall churchwardens to scratch his name out of their service books and their colleagues at Bungay to knock out windows and remove banners dedicated to that saint. At this time the clergy were encouraged to install English Bibles in their churches, partly at their own cost, but Hadleigh went further and illegally used English in the Mass—one of the first places in England to do so. In 1541, more ceremonies were forbidden, including the choosing of a Boy Bishop each December. This resulted, at a later date, in the sale of red coats (both motheaten) worn by the Boy Bishop at Boxford and Long Melford.

Related institutions such as chantries and gilds also lost their possessions to the king, at least temporarily, in 1545. Chantries were endowments for the daily celebrating of Mass for certain souls, often in a specially built chapel. The chantry priest was sometimes the village schoolmaster, as at Lavenham, Long Melford, Clare and Orford, so that his removal deprived the parish of an important service. Gilds, which were widespread in Suffolk, were social and religious societies. They were in many ways forerunners of 18th- and 19th-century friendly societies, but were never—apart, perhaps, from Bury and Ipswich—associated with crafts and trades. They existed in nearly every parish in the western half of the county, but were less common in what is now Suffolk Coastal District. There, in larger parishes like Framlingham and Woodbridge, each had a gild serving the surrounding area (illus. 70). Some of these rural gilds had petered out before the 1540s, but the closure of the survivors must have been a major loss in social life.

Henry VIII died in January 1547, an event which made way for the complete reformation of church practices. By means of orders issued later that year, all images and shrines were banished from parish churches, all processions (except the beating of the bounds) were banned, services were henceforth to be in Eng-

67 *Thomas Wolsey (c.1475-1530), son of an Ipswich trader, became archbishop, cardinal, lord chancellor, chief minister of Henry VIII and candidate for the papacy.*

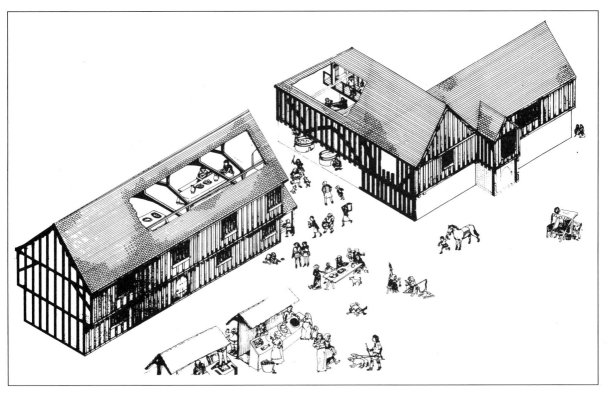

lish, and the elaborate equipment formerly used in worship was now redundant. So began the despoiling of the fine interiors of our churches, the achievement of centuries of medieval piety. Although church building in Suffolk seems mainly to have ceased by 1530 or so, apart from isolated exceptions such as Hawstead and Heveningham, the decoration of interiors, especially the painting and gilding of tabernacles and roodlofts, continued into the 1540s. This resplendent decoration was accompanied by colourful murals and finely carved and coloured roofs, and lit by numerous candles and candelabra. Yet practically everything had gone within two years of Henry's death.

The few churchwardens' accounts which survive for this period record the ripping out of images, tabernacles, roodlofts and altars, the scraping of paintings and the putting-up of biblical texts. Silver plate and valuables were sold—worth £100 in places like Beccles, Mildenhall and Southwold, compared with £30 at Lavenham and Woolpit, and under £10 in more than half the parishes in the county. The money was used for church repairs and other parish expenses including, at coastal places, sea defences, while any surplus was invested to assist the poor.

Chantries and gilds were finally abolished and their possessions taken by the Crown unless, as in the case of the Holy Ghost gild of Beccles, it could be shown that their activities were predominantly secular and not religious. In the final months of the reign, surviving pieces of plate and vestments were confiscated, leaving each parish with a single chalice and surplice.

68 *Debenham: reconstruction of Holy Trinity gildhall as in mid-15th century. The gildhall (left) which still exists, had an unheated banqueting hall on the first floor. On the right, the fraternity's 'Gylynghows' (brewhouse with vats) and other administrative or domestic rooms can be seen—this is now the* Red Lion.

69 *Shire Hall, Wood-bridge: court-room of Liberty of St Etheldreda, with market beneath. Basically Elizabethan, remodelled c.1700.*

In 1552, with the introduction of the second prayer book, the term 'mass' and the wearing of vestments were abandoned, and altars were replaced by tables set lengthwise (that is, east to west). By July 1553, when Edward died, the reformation of church worship was complete. The beliefs of Suffolk people seem also to have been changing, as only a small proportion of those making wills were still using the traditional language of 'Our Lady and all the saints'.

The accession of Queen Mary meant that the pattern was totally reversed. After an act repealing all the religious provisions of Edward's reign church-wardens had to set about re-equipping their churches for the return to Catholic worship, purchasing service books, cloths and banners, images and image-cloths, roods and roodlofts and many other items. In some places, such as Long Melford, several pieces of pre-Reformation equipment had been preserved in private hands and were merely moved back into the church; in others, as at Boxford, the churchwardens ran into debt with the cost of replacing them.

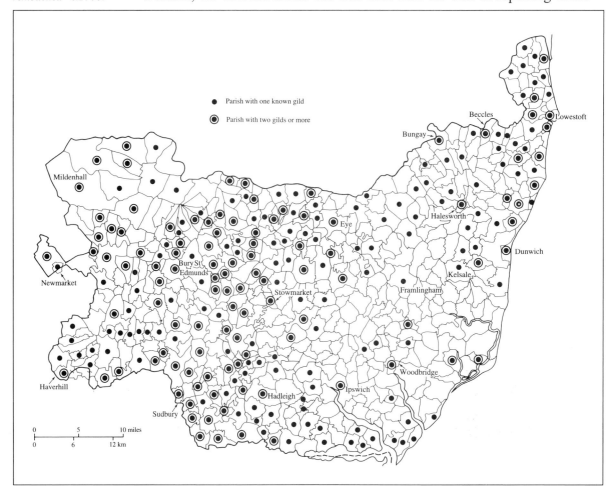

70 *Suffolk parishes known to have had medieval gilds: based on chantry certificates, tax returns and unfinished work on wills. Many parishes in the south-east supported gilds in Framlingham, Woodbridge and Kelsale.*

Dr. Taylor *rebuking a Popish Priest who was about to say Mass in Hadley Church.*

71 *Catholic versus Protestant in Suffolk: a later artist's reconstruction of a dramatic confrontation which led to the martyrdom of Dr. Rowland Taylor, Rector of Hadleigh, in 1555. From John Foxe's* Book of Martyrs, *edition of 1732.*

Because of this expense, and perhaps lack of conviction, refurbishing took time. Thus, at Bungay, Molle the sexton was paid for fixing the figures on the rood in 1558, only months before being paid to take them down again. Although Suffolk people seem, in the main, to have supported Mary as legitimate heir to the throne, they were not so sympathetic towards her religious beliefs. Their wills show only about one in four testators committed to Mary's Catholicism.

In retrospect, Queen Mary's reign is often seen as merely a hiccup in the progress of the Reformation. Yet, had Mary lived as long as her sister, the movement for reform might have been snuffed out. Some Protestants were certainly made to pay heavily for their beliefs in this period; nearly 30 individuals from Suffolk were martyred. It was no consolation to them that the lord chancellor responsible for re-introducing the law for burning them was Stephen Gardiner, a native of Bury St Edmunds. In addition, approximately a

72 *Mendlesham church: armour from the collection established in Elizabethan times.*

fifth of the clergy were deprived of their benefices, chiefly because they had married.

The Elizabethan settlement and its opponents

Towards the end of 1558, the accession of Queen Elizabeth signalled another round of destruction within churches. Almost immediately altars were broken up, roodlofts cut down and images and paintings removed. Successive acts, injunctions and proclamations, implemented by 'visitors' and commissioners, ensured that the protestant church of England was formally established by the early 1560s.

All, however, was not plain sailing. Although East Anglia did not have a strong Roman Catholic movement like that in the north, a number of important Suffolk families (more than 50 by the end of the reign) led by the Howards, Dukes of Norfolk, clung to their Catholicism and represented a threat to church and queen. They were kept in control by mainly protestant justices who imposed punitive fines for not attending church. Many substantial families, like the Bedingfields of Bedingfield, the Sulyards of Haughley Park and the Rokewoods of Euston and Stanningfield had large parts of their estates confiscated and leased out for the benefit of the Crown. Only in the Lothingland area, where the Jernegan family held sway, were recusants able to maintain their power and freedom for any length of time.

Two Suffolk recusants deserve special mention. Sir Thomas Cornwallis (1519-1604) was a distinguished royal servant who had been Comptroller of the Household to Queen Mary. When Elizabeth succeeded to the throne, he retired to his estates around Brome in Suffolk. Though he remained a Catholic, he was prepared to attend the parish church, and always proclaimed his loyalty to the queen. At intervals, his long retirement was punctuated by suspicions, interrogations, heavy fines and confinements in London. Ambrose Rokewood, the

73 *Brome: effigies of Sir Thomas Cornwallis and his wife. Sir Thomas (1519-1604) was comptroller of the household of Queen Mary, but lived in retirement at Brome throughout Elizabeth's reign. He was under regular suspicion as a Catholic or recusant.*

V *Clare: Norman chapel of Chilton Street, made into a house after the Reformation.*

To alle men present or in absence
Which to seynt Edmund haue deuocion
With hool herte and deth reuerence
Seyn this Antephne and this Orisson
Two hundred daies ys grauntid off pardoun
Wrete and registred afforn his hooly shryne
Which for our feith suffrede passioun
Blyssid Edmund kyng martir and virgyne

VI *Bury St Edmunds: shrine of St Edmund in the abbey, as depicted in John Lydgate's 'Life of St Edmund'.*

VII *Bradfield St George: medieval-style coppicing recently restored in Felshamhall Wood.*

VIII *Hawstead: the Camping Pightle adjacent to the church. Sites of this kind were used for camping, an early form of football, and other recreations.*

young squire of Stanningfield, was less of a survivor. He became involved in the Gunpowder Plot of 1605—chiefly, it was said, because of a fine stable of horses which his fellow conspirators wished to use.

At the other end of the religious spectrum were the Puritans, who felt that the Reformation had not gone far enough. They placed great emphasis on the quality and learning of the clergy and wanted the power of bishops curtailed. Clergy of this persuasion refused to use certain parts of the prayer book, to wear the surplice (originally enforced to prevent the wearing of other vestments) and to make the sign of the cross at baptism. In episcopal visitations of the 1590s, about a third (over 160) of the beneficed clergy in Suffolk were reported for not wearing the surplice, an indication of the strength of local Puritan feeling. Many clerical livings were in the gift of Puritan patrons, perhaps as many as 50 over the county as a whole, and they ensured that their nominees were like-minded. Sir Robert Jermyn of Rushbrooke and Sir John Higham of Barrow controlled about 15 benefices in this way.

74 *John Tradescant the elder (c.1570-1638), traveller and royal gardener, probably born at Corton.*

One of Suffolk's leading Puritans was John Knewstubb, rector of Cockfield. There, in 1582, he held a secret conference of over 60 clergy from Suffolk, Essex and Norfolk. The aim was to examine the prayer book, 'what might be tolerated and what necessarily to be refused'. Out of this grew other, more permanent conferences of Puritan clergy. One at Dedham, involving both Essex and Suffolk men, is well known because its minutes survive and are published. The east of the county, on the other hand, produced the unusual phenomenon of a gentleman-preacher, John Lawrence of South Elmham, acting as the leading Puritan light in that district. The reign of Elizabeth also saw the establishment of lectureships filled by puritan preachers who were appointed by magistrates, towns or individuals. They also held their own regular conferences. Preachers served not only the larger towns like Bury St Edmunds and Ipswich, but also small villages like Denham and Chedburgh. East Bergholt even managed to support three lecturers in addition to its incumbent.

The Puritanism of Elizabethan times led eventually to the development of separate nonconformist congregations. This was largely due to the uncompromising attitudes of Archbishop Whitgift and his successors who forced Puritan ministers out of the church instead of trying to absorb them. More than 50 Suffolk ministers were suspended in 1584 for refusing to subscribe to Whitgift's 'articles', and in the previous year two in the Bury area, John Copping and Elias Thacker, had been hanged, allegedly for denying the queen's supremacy.

Civil unrest

In spite of its reputation for good, stable government, Suffolk was not completely devoid of civil unrest in the 16th century. Steadily rising prices, combined with the decline of the broadcloth industry and increased taxation, led to considerable discontent among urban and rural workers. In 1525, a rising of some 4,000 in the area around Lavenham and Brent Eleigh, with reverberations in Bury and Cambridge, was put down by the diplomacy of the Dukes of Suffolk and Norfolk, working with the local gentry. Twenty-four years later, in 1549, unrest swept over the whole country resulting, in Norfolk, in what is known as

75 *Lavenham: Tudor shop-front, originally unglazed. The lower shutter was propped to form a counter.*

76 *Tunnel-like gateway to Erwarton Hall, probably Jacobean.*

77 *Suffolk industries of the 17th and 18th centuries: based on Richard Blome,* Britannia *(1673) and Anon.,* Description of England and Wales *(1769).*

Kett's rebellion. 'They have risen in every part of England', wrote the Spanish ambassador, 'asking for things both just and unjust.' The rebels set up camps near centres of local government, since their main grievance was the mismanagement of the ruling classes. In Suffolk camps were established at Bury St Edmunds and Melton (by Woodbridge), but the intervention of local noblemen, influential in government circles, seems to have prevented any real conflict. In Norfolk, on the other hand the use of military force led by 'foreigners' from other counties resulted in the famous pitched battle on Mousehold Heath.

In 1553, further risings were sparked off by the accession of Queen Mary, although practically all the gentry of east Suffolk swore their allegiance to her at Framlingham. The only other major disturbance in the area was in July 1569, when an abortive popular rebellion was attempted, chiefly around Lavenham. There a weaver, John Porter, who had also been involved in 1525, seems to have been the ringleader, stirring up ill feeling against *nouveaux riches*.

Industrial change

The troubles of 1525 had been chiefly due to a slackening of the cloth trade, which forced clothiers to give less work to spinners, weavers and finishers. This setback in the previously rich cloth trade was the first of many increasingly serious recessions in the 16th century. The industry had, by this time, spread

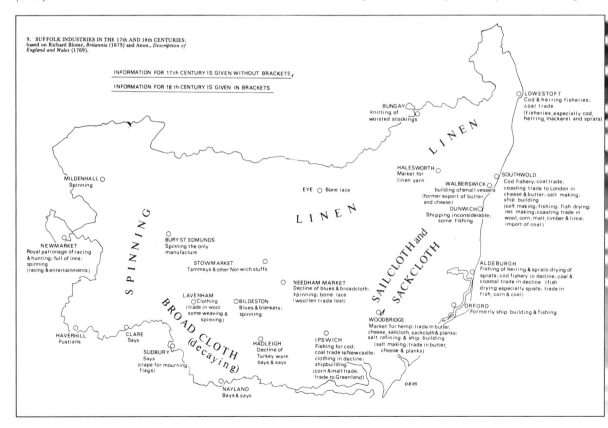

9. SUFFOLK INDUSTRIES IN THE 17th AND 18th CENTURIES:
based on Richard Blome, *Britannia* (1673) and Anon., *Description of England and Wales* (1769).

INFORMATION FOR 17th CENTURY IS GIVEN WITHOUT BRACKETS

INFORMATION FOR 18th CENTURY IS GIVEN IN BRACKETS

LOWESTOFT
Cod & herring fisheries;
coal trade
(fisheries, especially cod,
herring, mackerel and sprats)

BUNGAY
knitting of
worsted stockings

LINEN

HALESWORTH
Market for
linen yarn

WALBERSWICK
building of small vessels
(former export of butter
and cheese)

SOUTHWOLD
Cod fishery; coal trade;
coasting trade to London in
cheese & butter; salt making;
ship building
(salt making; fishing; fish drying;
net making; coasting trade in
wool, corn, malt, timber & lime;
import of coal)

DUNWICH
Shipping inconsiderable;
some fishing

EYE   Bone lace

LINEN

MILDENHALL
Spinning

SPINNING

NEWMARKET
Royal patronage of racing
& hunting; full of inns;
spinning
(racing & entertainments)

BURY ST EDMUNDS
Spinning the only
manufacture

STOWMARKET
Tammeys & other Norwich stuffs

NEEDHAM MARKET
Decline of blues & broadcloth;
spinning; bone lace
(woollen trade lost)

SAILCLOTH and SACKCLOTH

ALDEBURGH
Fishing of herring & sprats; drying of
sprats; cod fishery in decline; coal &
coastal trade in decline (fish
drying especially sprats; trade in
fish, corn & coal)

ORFORD
Formerly ship building & fishing

HAVERHILL
Fustians

CLARE
Says

LAVENHAM
Clothing
(trade in wool
some weaving &
spinning)

BILDESTON
Blues & blankets;
spinning

BROAD CLOTH (decaying)

SUDBURY
Says
(crape for mourning;
flags)

HADLEIGH
Decline of
Turkey ware,
bays & says

WOODBRIDGE
Market for hemp; trade in butter,
cheese, sailcloth, sackcloth & planks;
salt refining & ship building
(salt making; trade in butter,
cheese & planks)

IPSWICH
Fishing for cod;
coal trade to Newcastle;
clothing in decline;
shipbuilding
(corn & malt trade;
trade to Greenland)

NAYLAND
Bays & says

DB 85

ver a wider area outside the original centres in southern Suffolk. By the 1550s othiers were working in such places as Debenham, Badwell Ash and Felsham. ome of them were individually wealthy but the state of the cloth trade as a hole was steadily worsening. This reversal seems to have been due to several ctors: a falling demand for Suffolk dyed cloth on the European market, export strictions in this country, and the activities of specialist companies such as the lerchant Adventurers and the Eastland Company. The final blow to any hope f recovery in the late 16th century was the outbreak of war with Spain. By 522, clothiers had thousands of unsaleable cloths on their hands and were escribed as 'much decayed in their estates by reason of the great losses they ave received'.

The cloths that *did* become increasingly saleable at this time were the orsted-like 'new draperies' which, being lighter and generally more colourful, ommanded a wider market. Most districts which had produced broadcloth and her traditional fabrics failed to adapt to the new fashion, and this sealed their te. As a result, towns and villages which had been famed for woollen cloth, ich as Bury St Edmunds, Lavenham and East Bergholt, ended up merely pplying yarn to the weavers of Norwich and Essex. Only the occasional ace, such as Sudbury, Haverhill and Glemsford, took up the new fabrics and cured a new lease of manufacturing life.

78 *Arms of borough of Hadleigh, incorporated 1618. Notice the wool-sacks.*

79 *Orford Ness: the ever-shifting tip of the long shingle spit between the River Ore and the North Sea. The growth of this spit destroyed the prosperity of the medieval port of Orford.*

80 *Monument in Hadleigh church to Thomas Alabaster, clothier, died 1592.*

Coastal areas, too, suffered an eclipse. In the 15th century, Iceland and th North Sea had been highly profitable areas for both fishing and trading. Th wealth of those involved is reflected in fine churches, or their remains, all alor the coast. Decreasing demand for fish after the Reformation, combined wi increasing foreign competition and piracy, progressively limited the activity o of ports which were, anyway, fighting a losing battle with the advancing se By the end of the 16th century Dunwich haven was completely blocked, Orfo was 'now lying in the greatest ruin and decay' and, after 25 years of the ne century, Walberswick was said to be 'one of the poorest townes in Englan (illus. 58). On the other hand, Aldeburgh seems to have maintained its trad though steadily losing ground to the sea, and Southwold was thriving, despi its silting haven. Ship-building was also a prosperous trade in Ipswich ar Woodbridge.

Agriculture and landowning

Throughout this period, agriculture was booming. The enormous increase population—nearly doubling in the two centuries up to 1650—ensured a grov ing demand for food and caused its price to rise sevenfold. Wages, on the oth hand, only trebled, so providing increasing margins of profit for food producer This situation was largely responsible for the well-being of the rural gentry ar yeoman farmers. Their success is strongly reflected in the writing of the perio *The Chorography of Suffolk* (*c.*1603) stresses the flourishing state of dai farming in High Suffolk; Thomas Tusser in his *Five Hundred Points* (1570 firmly associates prosperity with the growing amount of enclosed land in th county; while Robert Reyce in his *Breviary* (*c.*1602) judges that frugal livir and thriftiness in a period of inflation caused the Suffolk yeomanry 'to gro with the wealth of this world'. Another factor in their favour was a buoya market in land, triggered off in the 1530s by the release and break-up monastic estates.

The sale by the Crown (only in rare instances, *gift*) of about 200 confiscate manors, together with a great deal of other land, enabled many Suffolk famili to increase their land holdings. The majority were already well established the county. Some, like the Duke of Norfolk, who acquired a larger number manors than any other individual, were of the nobility; some, like the Jermy and Bedingfields, were long-standing county gentry; while others, such as th Gosnolds and Chekes were well-to-do yeomen whose entrance into manori lordship sealed their rise to gentility. Others who strengthened their position this way were successful merchants like Kitson, Cullum and Alverd, and lav yers or crown servants such as Cordell and Winthrop. Perhaps the outstandir example was Nicholas Bacon, of yeoman stock, who at first was solicitor of th Court of Augmentations (which disposed of monastic property) and attorney the Court of Wards and Liveries. Later he became Lord Keeper of the Gre Seal, amassed extensive property and left a substantial country estate to eac of his five sons.

81 *A Suffolk yeoman: brass of Anthony Pettow (died 1610), Middleton church.*

ducation and charity

aw became, in Elizabethan times, the ultimate in higher education. Gentle-
en's sons were sent to Inns of Court at London after, or instead of, university.
rammar schools where boys were prepared for university, or at least teachers
f grammar, existed by this time in most Suffolk towns and in some villages.
he majority of these establishments were short-lived, run by individual masters
s a commercial proposition, but an increasing number, like those at Botesdale,
ungay and Eye, came to be endowed with charitable gifts on a permanent
asis. By the end of the 17th century, the great majority of the gentry were
terate, about 70 per cent of the yeomen and tradesmen, but only very few of
e county's remaining inhabitants. This was a great period for charitable giving
hen numerous bequests and donations were made towards the relief of the
oor. With a steadily growing population, especially in towns, poverty was a
ajor and escalating problem. In the 1520s, about 20 per cent of East Anglians
ved in towns, but 150 years later the figure had increased to over 30 per cent,
nd Ipswich had overtaken Bury St Edmunds as the largest town in Suffolk. By
600, about 90 places in Suffolk had charitable funds for the poor, and by the
iddle of the century another 50 places had the same. Sometimes these new
narities were combined with those of pre-Reformation times which certain
arishes had been able to snatch back from the royal commissioners. About 30
hools were included among these endowments. Ipswich, as might be ex-
ected, had by far the largest number of charities.

82 *Early poor-box carved from solid tree-trunk, iron-bound, set in floor of Kedington church.*

83 *Little Thurlow: the free school founded in 1614 by the local squire, a former Lord Mayor of London, to teach English, Latin and arithmetic to children in the district, without charge.*

84 *Eye: a jettied gildhall, probably early 16th-century, built on the edge of the churchyard; used as a grammar school after the Reformation.*

85 *Moot Hall, Aldeburgh: meeting-place of the Corporation since 16th century. Stands in remains of Market Place, close to the encroaching sea.*

Suffolk at sea

During Elizabethan and Jacobean times, Suffolk, as a maritime county, was naturally involved with international issues—foreign trade, piracy, war with Spain, colonisation and voyages of discovery. The sea-dogs of Suffolk, though less well-known than those of Devon, included John Eldred who made a fortune trading spices from Syria, and built Nutmeg Hall at Saxham; Thomas Cavendish of Trimley who, in 1586-8, became the second Englishman to circumnavigate the world; and Bartholomew Gosnold who discovered and named Cape Cod, Massachusetts, in 1602, and helped to found the first permanent settlement in North America at Jamestown in 1607. The feats of such men were chronicled by Richard Hakluyt, rector of Wetheringsett, in his *Principal Voyages and Discoveries of the English Nation*, first published in 1589.

86 *Walsham-le-Willows: Timothy Easton's reconstruction of the Game Place or open-air theatre, described in a survey of 1577. Such recreational arenas may have been commonplace, but only rarely are they mentioned in documents.*

6

War and Turmoil, 1630-1710

87 *Samuel Ward (1577-1640), town lecturer of Ipswich for over 30 years.*

In the 1630s, life in Suffolk seemed increasingly precarious and turbulent. The woollen industry was still deeply depressed, civil 'tumults' were constantly feared by the authorities, and recurrent outbreaks of plague threatened both town and country. Meanwhile, Suffolk was increasingly torn by social, religious and political controversy. The policies of Charles I, for example his refusal to convene parliament and his desperate attempts to raise money, caused mounting resentment among the wealthier and more articulate sections of society. Ship money was demanded annually after 1635, and Suffolk showed notable reluctance to pay. By 1640 only £200 was raised out of an annual assessment of about £8,000, and the sheriff, facing 'innumerable groans and sighs', declared himself almost ruined. The war against Scotland, which broke out in 1639, was also very unpopular, and led to a soldiers' mutiny at Bungay and a transport strike at Ipswich. When the king did at last reconvene parliament in 1640, strong parliamentarian candidates were swept into office like Sir Nathaniel Barnardiston of Kedington, Sir Simonds d'Ewes of Stowlangtoft and Sir Philip Parker of Arwarton.

At the same time, religious disputes increasingly threatened the unity of the Church of England. Puritan ministers, supported by growing numbers of the gentry and educated laity, expressed bitter dissatisfaction with normal Anglican compromises and with standards of personal and public morality. When William Laud was appointed Archbishop of Canterbury in 1633, and tried to impose his 'Popish' ideas of ritual and discipline, the situation became explosive.

Bishop Matthew Wren of Norwich, appointed in 1635, was one of Laud's strongest supporters. When staying at Ipswich in 1636, he found many defects in Suffolk and particularly objected to the influence of recalcitrant Puritan lecturers supported by town corporations and local gentlemen. He tried to impose a strong discipline and commanded, *inter alia*, the use of set prayers rather than informal ones, the railing in of communion tables 'under the east wall of the chancel', the use of surplices and hoods, the removal of hats during services, bowing at the name of Jesus and the licensing of private chaplains and tutors. Some clergy in the diocese were subsequently excommunicated, suspended or driven out, including Edmund Calamy, lecturer of Bury, and Samuel Ward, lecturer of Ipswich. In 1634 the latter was hauled before the court of High Commission where, among 43 charges, he was accused of praying informally and giving 'scandalous and offensive speeches in the pulpit'.

The turmoil of this period is best illustrated by the emigration of about 650 people from Suffolk to New England, mainly during the years 1629-38.

Motivated by both dissatisfaction and hope they, and about 1,200 others from Norfolk and Essex, were prepared to sell their homes, goods, and sometimes estates, and to risk a voyage of 3,000 miles across the Atlantic. N.C.P. Tyack has shown that the emigrants included husbandmen, yeomen, craftsmen (such as carpenters and weavers), clergy and gentry; they came from villages like Groton, Assington and Fressingfield, and from market towns and industrial centres like Lavenham, Sudbury and Bury St Edmunds.

One cause of disenchantment was certainly economic. Bishop Wren argued that 'poor workmen' were driven abroad by low wages, while John Winthrop, senior, a lawyer and landowner who became the first governor of Massachusetts, wrote about the effects of over-population, unemployment, poverty and petty crime. In an unforgettably sad phrase, he said that 'This Land (England) growes weary of her Inhabitants'. But religious disputes were of even greater significance, especially in the later 1630s. Each side blamed the other. Puritan ministers, especially Samuel Ward, were accused of encouraging 'this giddiness and desire to go to New England', while Bishop Wren was castigated for driving out God-fearing people by his popish idolatry. Clearly the chance of setting up a new and purified church on the other side of the Atlantic was the supreme attraction. 'I shall call that my country', said the younger John Winthrop, 'where I may most glorify God.'

The emigration got underway properly in 1630, when 112 men, women and children left Suffolk. They included John Winthrop, senior, of Groton, then aged 43, who went in the *Arbella* from Southampton with three members of his family and eight servants. His wife and three other children followed in 1631. In spite of the government's attempts to regulate and dissuade, the outflow continued throughout the 1630s. Within a few years the new plantations, their names often redolent of Suffolk and East Anglia, were claimed as highly successful. In the words of another Puritan squire who stayed behind, Sir Simonds d'Ewes, the emigrants had 'beyond the hopes of their friends, and to the astonishment of their enemies, raised such forts, built so many towns, brought into culture so much ground, and so dispersed and enriched themselves ... that the very finger of God hath hitherto gone with them and guided them'.

88 *Font-cover at Mendlesham, 1630.*

The Civil Wars

In 1642 the king raised his standard at Nottingham, and the first Civil War began. Almost immediately, parliament ordered a group of Suffolk gentlemen to seize the county magazine at Bury St Edmunds, and a protestant mob from the area around Colchester and Sudbury attacked Catholic homes. They began with the house of Countess Rivers at St Osyth and, when she escaped to her other mansion at Long Melford, ransacked that too. The Countess managed to escape with her life, but had allegedly lost goods to the value of £50,000. Other Catholic families to suffer from this violence included the Martins at Melford Place and the Mannocks of Stoke by Nayland.

In Suffolk, the only significant military event in the first war was the so-called siege of Lowestoft in March 1643, which showed how quickly and decisively Oliver Cromwell could act. Hearing that Lowestoft had been occu-

89 *Somerleyton Hall: oak carving in style of Grinling Gibbons.*

HERE LYETH ROGER MARTVN OF LONGMELE
FORD ESQVIER, WHO DYED THE THIRD DAY
OF AVGVST IN THE YEARE OF OVR LORD
1615 AND IN 89ᵗ ʸᴱᴬᴿᴱ OF HIS AGE

90 *Long Melford: the brass of Roger Martin and his two wives. He wrote an invaluable description of Melford church as it was before the Reformation.*

pied by Royalist gentry, he rode from Cambridge with 1,000 horse, surprised the opposition completely, and took the town without a fight. In the absence, therefore, of serious fighting on Suffolk soil, the main interest of the war was administrative and financial. The country had been so alienated by the high-handed and insensitive policies of Charles I that its ruling class had little difficulty in declaring for parliament, and in organising the county's considerable resources for that cause.

Not that Suffolk was without Royalists. At least 50 gentry families supported the king, many actually joining his army, and Royalist sentiment was always likely to erupt in certain places. For example, the newly established races at Newmarket were said to be a cover for Royalist disaffection, and the Jermyn family at Rushbrooke provided a focus in the Bury area. In 1646 a Puritan attempt to suppress the celebration of Christmas in Bury led to a popular riot which was seen as a 'horrible plot and bloody conspiracy'. Although not numerous, the Royalists of Suffolk paid large sums of money in fines. Between 1643 and 1649, their sequestered estates yielded £40,917—more than was got from any other English county. Many Suffolk people must have been reluctant to take sides, and hated the spectre of civil war, but they never organised themselves as a middle party. So, with the Royalists driven underground, the rule of the parliamentary party was virtually unchallenged.

During the war, Suffolk was controlled by an unpaid county committee which met regularly at Bury. Its membership, remarkably stable from 1642 to the Restoration in 1660, included members of principal families who were already used to governing as magistrates and deputy lieutenants, such as Sir William Spring of Pakenham, Sir John Wentworth of Somerleyton and Sir John Rous of Henham. Whether they attended regularly or not, members were under the firm leadership of Sir Nathaniel Barnardiston of Kedington who was the wealthiest man in the county (illus. 91). (Incidentally, a Barnardiston was said to have been the original 'Roundhead'.) In the words of Alan Everitt, 'the Committee of Suffolk was in fact a kind of exclusive county club comprising most of the brains and much of the wealth of the shire'. Such people were economically experienced as landowners and businessmen, and they were already deeply imbued with Puritan ideas. As Robert Reyce wrote, about 40 years before the Civil War, Suffolk gentlemen thought of themselves as 'crowned with the purity of true religion and godly life'.

91 Kedington: effigies of Sir Nathaniel Barnardiston and his wife. He was the strong-minded leader of the Puritan oligarchy who ruled Suffolk during the Civil War and Commonwealth. He died in 1653 and she in 1669.

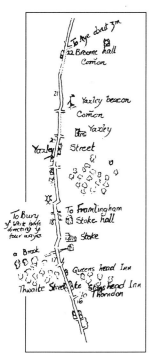

92 *Part of strip-map in John Ogilby's* Britannia *(1675) showing Pye Street, the modern A140.*

The primary function of the committee was to raise troops, horses and money for the parliamentary cause. During the period 1642-48 they efficiently collected an average of over £56,000 a year. In February 1643 Suffolk joined the Eastern Association of five, later seven, counties. At first this alliance was purely defensive and each county jealously guarded its independence, but from August 1643 the Earl of Manchester exerted a much firmer discipline. Nevertheless, it was not until January 1644 that *offensive* warfare became a real possibility. Then, after originally rejecting the idea, the eastern counties accepted the concept of a New Model Army. This reorganisation led, within two years, to the decisive victory of Naseby. In the estimation of Alan Everitt, 'it would be but a slight rhetorical exaggeration to say that London and the Eastern Association had conquered England'.

But how did the Civil War affect the ordinary parish and its inhabitants? From miscellaneous records, we get occasional glimpses of local activities: parishes raising troops, offering volunteers, sending soldiers for training, buying and repairing arms and armour, and relieving sick and injured soldiers. In March 1643, the small village of Shimpling provided five volunteers for the Eastern Association, and collected money, seven muskets, a sword and an old helmet.

Undoubtedly, the lives of some individuals were completely changed by the war. Ralph Margery of Walsham-le-Willows was a substantial local yeoman or, at best, a minor gentleman. Being a convinced Puritan, he volunteered to fight against the king, collected horses locally, raised his own troop, and rose to be captain. It was of Margery that Cromwell wrote those famous words, 'I had rather have a plain russet-coated captain that knows what he fights for and loves what he knows than any gentleman'. His men became the 13th Troop of Ironsides and fought at Naseby. Margery went on to serve as a professional soldier in Scotland and the Channel Isles, but died back home at Walsham in 1653.

Unlike Essex which witnessed the bloody siege of Colchester, Suffolk was little affected by the second Civil War of 1648-49. The so-called Royalist rebellion at Bury in 1648, when over 600 people are said to have danced around a maypole, was a spontaneous eruption of Royalist and anti-Puritan sentiment, but it was never a serious military threat. With little bloodshed, the Parliamentary army regained the town within two days.

Church and chapel

The Long Parliament, which first met in November 1640, introduced major changes in religion. Bishops were summarily abolished and the Book of Common Prayer proscribed. In March 1644, two committees were appointed to remove anti-Puritan clergy in west and east Suffolk. Local parishioners, whose social standing varied, gave evidence showing that ministers were either 'scandalous' (Laudian or ritualistic), 'malignant' (Royalist) or simply immoral. As a result, about 100 Suffolk incumbents were ejected and had to seek an alternative way of life, ranging precariously from teaching to beggary. Many of the charges against them were gossipy and malicious, but they make fascinating reading—witness Lionel Playters, rector of Uggeshall, who was accused of 'eating custard after a scandalous manner' and of offering his crop of hemp 'to hang up the Roundheads'.

In 1641 parliament had ordered that all superstitious pictures and inscriptions in churches be removed and defaced. The effect was not felt in Suffolk until 1644 when William Dowsing, who came from a Laxfield family, was appointed Parliamentary Visitor. In less than 50 days, accompanied by troopers, he personally swept through more than 150 Suffolk churches, while his deputies tackled the rest. In a few months, they destroyed countless religious objects which had escaped earlier purges. At Hacheston alone, Dowsing himself attacked 21 winged cherubim, 16 'superstitious pictures and popish saints', a double cross, a carving of the Holy Trinity on the font, emblems of the Passion, three stone crosses, and several stained-glass windows and steps in the chancel.

93 *Kedington church: canopied pulpit, reading desk and clerk's desk, known collectively as a three-decker pulpit. Note also the hour-glass and wig-pole.*

Contemporary superstitions and fear of magic were seen at their worst in the treatment of so-called witches. Although persecution was never as great and sustained as on the continent, it appeared sporadically in England throughout Elizabethan and Stuart times. The worst period for Suffolk was undoubtedly during the first Civil War when Matthew Hopkins, a native of the county, assumed the title of Witchfinder General. He toured the eastern counties, extorting confessions from suspects, or discovering witches by searching and torture. At Aldeburgh, financial accounts show that Hopkins persuaded the corporation to pay 'search women' for giving evidence, and to erect a special gallows. Seven witches were hanged, and the witchfinder was paid £2 for his trouble. In Suffolk as a whole, over 100 individuals were accused, and at least 60 of them were executed.

Most of the victims were elderly women of strange appearance and quirky habits who had fallen out with their neighbours. Susan Marchant of Hintlesham confessed to making a neighbour's cow lame, to having consorted with the devil, and to possessing three 'familiars' or 'imps'. The worst case was the rare persecution of a local clergyman, John Lowes, the 80-year-old vicar of Brandeston. Unfortunately he had antagonised his parishioners who were persuaded by the malevolent Hopkins to regard him as a witch. The old man was kept awake for several nights, forced to run until he was breathless and then 'swum' in a pond. He finally confessed to having two imps and was duly hanged.

In 1647 Hopkins' cruel methods were exposed, and he himself was put to death. Nevertheless, the killing of witches continued. Two widows from Lowestoft were tried at Bury in 1664. Their trial, which is well recorded, was an extraordinary farrago of witnesses struck dumb, witness physically attacking defendant, a lame child miraculously restored to health, and tales of exploding toads and children coughing up pins and nails. The accused were eventually found guilty and hanged. After the reign of Charles II, witches were no longer put to death, but they were still feared and occasionally punished. At Wickham Skeith, a local 'wizard' was dragged through the village pond as late as 1825.

94 *Walpole: one of the earliest surviving Nonconformist chapels in England.*

The Puritan victory of the early 1640s led to a restructuring of the church on Presbyterian lines. In 1645 Suffolk was divided into 14 'classical presbyteries' presided over by committees of ministers and laymen, in place of former deaneries and archdeaconries. The imposition of this new hierarchy, loosely based on the Scottish model, was largely a paper exercise. The victory of parliament over the king generated a ferment of new religious and political ideas, as the more extreme Protestants, in spite of Presbyterian persecution, broke away from the national church and successfully established their own meetings. This is excellently illustrated by the extraordinary career of Laurence Clarkson who frequently preached in Suffolk: between 1640 and 1658 he moved in and out of seven different 'churches' including Anglican, Baptist and Ranter, and finished up as a Muggletonian believing that mankind was divided into the seed of Adam who are saved and the seed of Cain who are automatically damned.

95 *Walpole: interior of Congregational chapel, one of England's oldest places of nonconformist worship. The congregation existed by 1647, and probably adapted this building from an earlier private house. Notice the simple benches, galleries, wooden columns and central pulpit.*

By far the most important of the new groups were the Independents (or Congregationalists) who, as descendants of the Elizabethan Brownists, believed that each congregation should be entirely self governing. They established groups in many parts of Suffolk, meeting mainly in private houses and outbuildings. Walpole chapel, converted from a private house, is claimed to be the oldest surviving nonconformist meeting-place in England, perhaps in use from the early 1640s (illus. 95). In 1646 a new Independent church in Bury was set up with the help of London missionaries called Katherine and Samuel Chidley: eight members signed a binding covenant. Of less importance numerically were the Baptists who rejected infant baptism and the Quakers who denied any form

of ministry between God and man. All these sects were treated harshly by the Presbyterian majority, particularly the Quakers who seemed to present both a religious and social threat. In 1657 George Whitehead, a Quaker preacher from Westmorland, was ordered to be whipped at Nayland 'till his body be bloody'. Two years later, George Fox of Charsfield called the Younger to distinguish him from the founder of Quakerism, faced a drawn sword and gun at Tunstall, was ejected and imprisoned for preaching in the market at Aldeburgh, preached four days later in the church ('steeple house') of Southwold, and was duly beaten by a mob and again imprisoned.

The permanent cleavage between 'church' and 'chapel' came later. In 1660 the Church of England, with its characteristic liturgy and government by bishops, was fully restored. In Suffolk about 25 clergy were ejected, either because they would not submit to discipline, or to restore men who had been dispossessed in the 1640s and were still alive. John King was deposed as vicar of Debenham; he took to farming, and gathered an Independent congregation around him (in spite of being imprisoned for a time). Similarly, Henry Sampson lost his posts as rector of Framlingham and Fellow of Pembroke College, Cambridge. He went to Padua to study medicine and subsequently became a notable dissenter in London.

96 *St Stephen's, Ipswich: monument to Robert Leman, died 1637.*

Licences granted during a brief period of toleration in 1672 illustrate the distribution of nonconformity. Most of the 39 licences to Presbyterians were in the south and west of the county, with a noticeable concentration in the Gipping valley, while most of the 31 licences to Congregationalists were in the north-east from Debenham across to Lowestoft. Bungay appears to have been an early centre for Baptists, though they did not achieve their greatest influence until the 19th century.

The size of individual congregations is revealed by the Compton Census of 1676, which survives for western Suffolk. Wattisfield, still a nonconformist centre, already had 49 Independents who lived under the protection of a local squire, Samuel Baker. The fact that a neighbouring parish, Hepworth, had another 37 dissenters shows how such congregations were 'gathered' from several places. At the same time, nonconformity appeared particularly strong in towns: Mildenhall had 66 dissenters, Sudbury about 100, Bury 167 and Clare as many as three hundred. At Lawshall one man bravely declared himself an atheist. In certain places like Stanningfield, Melford and Wetherden, the census also identified small groups of recusants, usually built around the households of known Catholic gentry—such as the Rokewoods, Martins and Sulyards.

Permanent toleration did not come about until 1689. Thereafter, nonconformity became an established and respectable element in Suffolk society, and many permanent chapels were built. Travellers in the early 18th century often commented on nonconformist enthusiasm, particularly in the larger towns. At Southwold in 1722, Daniel Defoe described a service in the church with only 27 worshippers, while the nearby Congregational chapel was 'full to the very doors' with over 600 people.

After James II was deposed by the Glorious Revolution of 1688, yet another group of the clergy was ousted—the so-called Non-jurors. Having already given

97 *William Sancroft (1617-93), Archbishop of Canterbury, deprived of office because a Nonjuror, buried at Fressingfield.*

allegiance to James, they felt unable to swear a new oath to William III. William Sancroft, Archbishop of Canterbury, was the most distinguished victim. He was ejected, and spent the last two years of his life in pious retirement in his native village of Fressingfield, where he was buried in 1693. Over twenty Suffolk clergy lost their livings at this time.

The Restoration

The restoration of Charles II in 1660 brought important changes of emphasis to Suffolk life. The high, unbending morality of Puritanism was relaxed at all levels of society. At the same time, much more interest was shown in secular subjects such as the improvement of agriculture, estate-management, commerce and transport. Political and religious debate was revived by the policies of the later Stuart kings, and quickly led to the emergence of new political parties.

Broadly speaking, the Whigs represented moneyed interests and favoured low-church Anglicanism, toleration for nonconformists and constitutional kingship; the Tories represented landed interests, tended to be high-church Anglicans and believed in the Divine Right of Kings. However, the political situation was always complicated and highly volatile, and depended as much on personalities as on policies. At first the Whigs of Suffolk seemed to have the upper hand, and they owed much to the influence of Sir Samuel Barnardiston of Brightwell. By Queen Anne's reign, however, the political pendulum had swung the other way. Under the leadership of Sir Robert Davers of Rushbrooke, the third Earl of Dysart of Helmingham, and Sir Thomas Hanmer of Mildenhall, the Tories won control of the two county seats, which were always the most prestigious, and substantially retained that control for much of the 18th century. Already the majority of the county's 5,000 or more voters, who greatly outnumbered the voters of the boroughs, were showing the Toryism which has remained a dominant factor in Suffolk's political life to the present day.

The life of Stuart Suffolk was dominated by a numerous upper-class of aristocracy and gentry. Alan Everitt calculates that, at the outbreak of the Civil Wars, Suffolk had 800-1,000 gentry; they included professionals such as doctors, lawyers and clergy, as well as the younger sons of landed families—in fact, anyone who called himself 'Esquire', 'Mister' or simply 'Gentleman'. In 1673 Richard Blome listed 342 nobility and gentry who probably represented the cream of county society, and certainly most of the landed interest.

The Hearth Tax returns of 1674 revealed 18 very large houses in Suffolk, each with 30 or more hearths. Top of the list came Hengrave Hall, home of the Gages, with 51 hearths, followed by Melford Hall where the Cordells had 49 hearths and Brome Hall (now gone) where the Cornwallises had 45 hearths. Ninety-five other houses owned by nobility or gentry had between 15 and 30 hearths. Most of these mansions had grown out of earlier manor houses. Indeed, architecturally most of them were medieval or Tudor houses which had been expanded or altered to suit changing tastes and rising status. Even Lord Arlington's great 'palace' at Euston was, in fact, an elaborate refacing and reorganising of the Elizabethan manor house built by the Rokewoods.

98 *Ancient House, Ipswich: Suffolk's finest example of ornamental plaster-work, c.1670.*

IX *Framlingham: remains within the great castle of the Bigods, later converted to the parish workhouse.*

X *Hengrave Hall: ornate oriel over the main entrance to Sir Thomas Kytson's mansion built in the early 16th century.*

XI *Shrubland Park: steps of the Italianate terraced gardens designed by Sir Charles Barry in the mid-19th century.*

XII *Buxhall: typical association of medieval church and rectory. The latter was long occupied by the 'squarson' family of Copinger.*

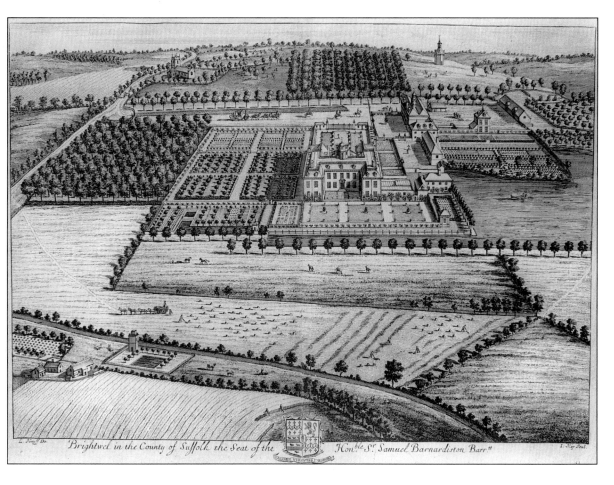

Brightwel in the County of Suffolk the Seat of the Hon.ble S.r Samuel Barnardiston Bar.tt

Local society was, of course, never static. Admittedly, some families such as the Playters of Sotterley and the Poleys of Boxted, had been resident gentry since the Middle Ages, and seemed to jog along happily on their ancestral estates. Others, however, by misfortune or miscalculation declined or failed. Good examples are the Gosnolds of Otley and the Glemhams of Little Glemham who, as royalists, never recovered from the punishments and financial penalties suffered in the period 1640-60. Alternatively, as in the 16th century, many genteel families were new arrivals who had been successful in marriage, trade and politics, the law or military service—thanks often to the ability and drive of a single individual. A few instances will serve: the Cullums of Hawstead and Blois family of Grundisburgh and Yoxford had been merchants in London and abroad; William Crofts of Little Saxham was rewarded with a baronetcy for political services to the Crown; and Thomas Allin, a merchant and shipowner of Lowestoft ended his career as an admiral and naval hero, with a seat at Somerleyton.

Suffolk's most important focus of social and political life, after the Restoration of Charles II, was undoubtedly Euston Hall. Between 1666 and 1670 the

99 Brightwell Hall: built, or remodelled, c.1663, by Sir Samuel Barnardiston, Bart., leader of the Suffolk Whigs in the later 17th century; demolished c.1760. Notice formal layout of gardens and farm; parts of the latter survive. Engraving published by J. Kip in 1707. (Allow for artistic licence: e.g. simultaneous gathering of corn and hay!)

house was expensively remodelled by its new owner, Sir Henry Bennett, later Earl of Arlington. He fought for Charles I in the Civil War, then joined the exiled court of Charles II in Paris and later acted as his representative in Madrid. After the king's restoration in 1660, he became Secretary of State, one of the so-called 'Cabal' of leading politicians. Fortunately, John Evelyn visited Euston in Arlington's day, and recorded the experience in his diary. In October 1671, Charles II paid a visit with the Duke of York (later James II) and a large train of followers. 'Came all the greate men from Newmarket and other parts both of Suffolk and Norfolk, to make their court, the whole house filled from one end to the other with lords, ladies and gallants.' With the help of about 100 servants, Arlington lavishly entertained at least 200 guests for 15 days.

Many facets of Restoration life are revealed by Evelyn's account: for instance, the new sexual morality, including the seduction of an un-named young lady, and the concern for field sports like hawking and stag hunting, card playing, gambling and horse riding. Like so many successful men, Arlington had 'gotten vastly but spent it hastily', running himself into considerable debt. Not only did he remodel

100 *Euston Park: the remains of a formal axis created by Lord Arlington and John Evelyn in the early 1670s. On the skyline, two clumps are the sawn-off ends of an avenue which originally straddled the whole valley, in line with the Hall itself. Only the left-hand half of the original house survives. The arch, planned by William Kent in the 1730s, was probably built several decades later.*

the Hall, employing Antonio Verrio to paint the ceilings of the state rooms, but he laid out formal pleasure gardens with walks, ponds and a canal, designed a huge park of 2,000 acres, dominated by a great avenue of trees aligned on the house, remodelled the parish church, consolidated the village on its present site, provided a new rectory and inn, and repaired the farms of his tenants. His only daughter Isabella was married to one of the king's illegitimate children, Henry Fitzroy, first Duke of Grafton. On Arlington's death in 1685 the estate passed to Isabella and Henry, and their descendants still live there today.

International Warfare

In the late 17th century, England and Holland came into increasing conflict over trade and fisheries, and this led to three separate wars between 1651 and 1674.

The Suffolk coast and adjoining waters were the scenes of several major engagements. In June 1665, a fierce naval battle was fought off Lowestoft, when an English fleet commanded by the Duke of York sank or captured 32 Dutch ships for the loss of two English ships. In July 1667, over 1,000 Dutch soldiers and seamen landed at Felixstowe—the last time an enemy force invaded English soil. While some of them engaged the Suffolk militia on Felixstowe cliffs, others attacked Landguard Fort. They were twice repelled, and the whole force had to withdraw during the night. In May 1672 the Battle of Sole Bay was fought off Southwold between the English and French fleets on the one side and the Dutch on the other. The noise of the guns was heard well inland and smoke drifted as far as the Essex coast, but the result was indecisive. After this and other battles in the North Sea, hundreds of wounded men and prisoners were brought ashore, particularly to Ipswich.

101 *Butter Cross at Bungay, built 1689 after a serious fire.*

7

Georgian Suffolk, 1710-1800

This period, between two very stormy ones, is not so obviously dominated by great national events nor, at a local level, is it particularly well-documented. It does, however, present opportunities of looking at how people actually lived, how local institutions worked and how new economic trends were beginning to change society.

Poverty

102 *Unitarian chapel, Ipswich: chandelier of early 18th century, probably by a Dutch craftsman.*

Poverty was now a major threat which required constant attention. The returns for the Hearth Tax of 1674 had already shown that many communities had a third or half of their inhabitants classified as poor. At Walberswick, as many as 61 per cent of local people were listed as too poor to pay the tax. Since 1674 the manufacture of Suffolk woollens had further declined, and many small farmers had sold out under pressure from bad harvests, low prices, indebtedness and the expansionist policies of their richer neighbours. To cope with poverty, a complicated system had been set up by Tudor and Stuart legislation. Each parish regularly levied rates on occupiers of land, and elected overseers of the poor who worked with churchwardens and constables. Many paupers were given relief in their own homes, or in kind. At East Bergholt, the overseers dispensed not only cash but clothing such as shoes, shirts and petticoats, and working equipment such as spinning wheels and woolcombing cards. They also apprenticed pauper children, paid for the services of doctors and nurses and organised the buying and distribution of fuel for the winter months. In the last resort, the parish paid for a pauper's funeral including coffin, bell, watchers, layers-forth and bearers.

As the 18th century wore on, a growing number of parishes provided their own workhouses, either purpose-built or adapted from an existing building. These establishments, under the control of specially appointed masters, gave shelter and employment to those who were unable otherwise to cope. By 1766, 94 Suffolk parishes had their own workhouses. The main concentrations were in Ipswich which had 13, and in the declining industrial districts of the south. In size they varied considerably: Melford's workhouse could accommodate 150 paupers but Somerleyton's only three. In the next 60 years or so the number of parish workhouses continued to grow. A fair proportion of these can be identified with surviving buildings, and more await discovery. At Brandon, for example, a handsome workhouse built in the early 18th century, still survives as church rooms; at Hadleigh, the famous medieval gildhall was adapted for the purpose. In 1783, Assington built a new workhouse, which still survives, at a cost of £230 (illus. 117). An inventory of 1808 shows that the Ward Room contained tables, stools, chairs, a coal range and 18 spinning wheels to keep the inmates busy.

Contemporaries soon appreciated the economic advantage of providing larger workhouses for *groups* of parishes. As early as 1747 James Vernon, a local landowner, left a farmhouse at Great Wratting as a workhouse for four contiguous parishes. From the 1750s, the eastern half of Suffolk was one of the first rural areas in England to provide large workhouses for whole 'hundreds'. The first was built in 1757 at Nacton to serve the Incorporated Hundreds of Carlford and Colneis: it could accommodate 350 paupers. Eight more such houses were built between 1756 and 1781. Architecturally they were imposing and good examples can still be seen at Onehouse near Stowmarket and Shipmeadow near Beccles. Meanwhile the urban parishes of Bury and Sudbury also combined to support centralised workhouses. Ipswich, however, retained its 13 separate workhouses until 1834.

By an act of 1662, each pauper was regarded as the responsibility of that parish where he had legal 'settlement'. Four basic qualifications could be claimed: by birth, by payment of rates above £10, by hired service for a full year, or by a full term as apprentice. Where an individual had claims on more than one parish, it was the *latest* which counted. Women gained the settlement of their husbands, and children that of their father. The Suffolk Record Office has thousands of documents resulting from this system, in particular removal orders by which those requiring relief were transported to their last place of legal settlement; settlement certificates which guaranteed that a pauper would be accepted by his place of settlement; and examinations which recorded interviews of paupers by local JPs.

The amount of human suffering and the actual effectiveness of relief are much harder to assess. At some periods, the attitudes of overseers and rate-payers were undoubtedly harsh—for example, from 1697, the poor were required by law to wear badges. Nor were the Incorporated Hundreds necessarily popular among the poor, for in 1765 the newly built workhouse at Bulcamp was attacked by an angry mob. In 1783 George Crabbe described the sad, forsaken and disabled inmates of the squalid parish workhouse at his native Aldeburgh.

Yet genuine concern and compassion can occasionally be glimpsed. In 1711, the officers of Castle Hedingham in Essex wrote to Walsham-le-Willows about Tim Fair and his family who were ultimately Walsham's responsibility. This family was considered to be frugal and industrious, but had been afflicted by the mother's poor health and the father's lack of work. Their neighbours in Essex had already made a collection for them. Without threatening removal, Castle Hedingham was keeping Walsham informed of the family's situation and inviting their co-operation.

Politics

In the 18th century Suffolk returned 16 MPs, two for the county itself and 14 (two each) for the boroughs of Aldeburgh, Bury St Edmunds, Dunwich, Eye,

103 *Sudbury: statue of the painter Thomas Gainsborough (1727-88), native of the town.*

104 *3rd Duke of Grafton (1735-1811), Prime Minister from 1767-70.*

Ipswich, Orford and Sudbury. About 7,000 people had the vote out of a total adult male population of approximately 38,000. By far the most numerous group was the 5,000 or more freeholders who elected the county MPs. By contrast the two members who represented Bury were chosen by the town's corporation, an electorate of only thirty-seven.

As in other parts of England, some boroughs were controlled by major landowning families. Until 1747 the Earl of Bristol virtually nominated Bury's MPs, and the corporation were happy to vote accordingly—especially when they were handsomely entertained at the earl's expense. Afterwards the patronage was shared between the earl and the Duke of Grafton. Eye was a 'pocket borough' too, controlled by the Cornwallis family; Dunwich fell to Sir George Downing when he bought a local estate; Orford in the 1730s was captured by the government which then spent £3,000 on houses for the free accommodation of voters. In other boroughs, however, elections could be decided by the corporations themselves, either by creating new freemen (as at Ipswich which had an electorate of over 500), or by making themselves available to the highest bidder. Thus Aldeburgh usually elected wealthy strangers who were expected to spend money on the borough. By the mid-18th century Sudbury was already said to be 'very venal—it may be had by money'.

Great houses and estates

The social landscape of 18th-century Suffolk was dominated by country houses and stately homes. All over the county, landowning gentry and aristocracy were investing heavily in building. Miles Barne, MP for Dunwich, bought Sotterley in 1744, demolished the old house of the Playters and built a new red-brick hall with pediments, Corinthian columns and fine fireplaces (illus. 105). The greatest of the county's Georgian mansions is Heveningham Hall, built for Sir Gerard Vanneck, a merchant of Dutch descent; it was designed *c*.1778 by Sir Robert Taylor and finished internally by James Wyatt. On the other hand, the two aristocrats who presided over county society, and who might have built Palladian mansions to rival Norfolk's Holkham and Houghton, got no further than contemplation. The first Earl of Bristol talked to Vanburgh about a new house at Ickworth but, faced with the extravagances of his family, did no more than modernise and extend a former farmhouse. At Euston, the 2nd Duke of Grafton was tempted by a new design from William Kent, but finally contented himself with Matthew Brettingham's modernising of the old hall.

Indeed, the majority of owners chose merely to remodel their existing houses by putting on Georgian fronts and reorganising internal spaces. At this time, many Elizabethan and Jacobean porches, pinnacles and transomed windows must have disappeared behind new façades with pediments, porticos and sash-windows. Dudley North, one of Suffolk's leading Tories, substantially altered his Tudor house at Little Glemham in 1720; slightly later, Richard Powys, MP for Orford, transformed the old Elizabethan hall of the Timperleys at Hintlesham.

The country house was not simply a residence. It was surrounded by gardens and parkland which provided ornament and the opportunity for walking, riding and field sports. Hodskinson's fine map of Suffolk, published in 1783, is dotted

105 *Sotterley Hall, church and park: the Hall was rebuilt c.1744, when the Barne family replaced the Playters who had lived there since the 15th century. The flanking screen-walls were added c.1820. The church is the only building of the medieval village to survive in the landscaped park. An engraving published by Henry Davy in 1824.*

with over 70 parks of varying sizes (illus. 109). They were particularly thick in the west of the county, near the coast and around the social capitals of Bury and Ipswich. By contrast, the centre-east, the homeland of the yeomanry since at least the 15th century, was still relatively empty.

Suffolk can still show a few examples of the geometrical and formal type of landscaping which was fashionable from 1660 to 1730. At Euston, part of a straight avenue of trees, originally over two miles long and focusing on the house itself, can still be seen (illus. 100); Campsey Ash has an excellent example of a long straight 'canal', its sides revetted in brick; at Ickworth the first earl's delightful summer house still nestles in walled gardens beside another canal, later naturalised (illus. 107). John Kip's engravings of Brome and Brightwell (illus. 99) in their heydays show such formal layouts in their entirety.

From about 1730, the new English style took root. Parks, invariably man-made, began to look more 'natural' with winding rivers and lakes, large plantations and clumps of trees, and great sweeps of grassland. The best-known of landscape designers, 'Capability' Launcelot Brown, left his mark on more than six places in Suffolk. One of the last parks on which he worked was at Heveningham. In 1784, when François de la Rochefoucauld visited Sir Gerard Vanneck, he was shown a small stream which, following Brown's plans, was about to be dammed and converted into 'a magnificent artificial river which

106 *Rotunda of Ickworth built 1796 to c.1830 for 4th Earl of Bristol, Bishop of Derry.*

107 *Ickworth: the 'canal' and summer-house created* c.*1715 by the 1st Earl of Bristol at his 'peaceful bless'd Ickworth'. Beyond are the medieval church beside which lay the original village and manor house, and the Rotunda of the 4th Earl's great mansion begun in 1796.*

promises ... to have a very natural appearance'. Humphry Repton succeeded Brown as England's leading landscaper. Examples of his famous Red Books, in which he summarised and illustrated his proposals for clients, survive for Culford, Henham and Tendring.

Beyond the park lay an area of farmland which was the economic base to the whole system. The owner either farmed it himself, from a Home Farm, or let the land to tenants in return for rent. An estate might range from a few hundred acres belonging to a local squire, to huge agglomerations containing thousands of acres. The Euston estate was said, in 1820, to have a circumference of 40 miles. This included six parishes and parts of several others. The Home Farm contained 3,200 acres and the whole estate, by 1873, stood at 13,643 acres. The finest farm in the county was said by Arthur Young to be Westwood Lodge at Blythburgh, the property of Sir John Blois. The house was the former lodge of a park or warren, converted into a farmhouse in 1637. From it a tenant farmed about 3,000 acres of light land which, by enclosure, marling and dunging, had been made highly productive.

108 *Bust of George Crabbe (1754-1832), poet and native of Aldeburgh.*

Ever since the Restoration of Charles II, the market in country houses and agricultural land had been buoyant. Men with money (or credit) were keen to buy land, not because it was necessarily a good investment but because it conferred status, influence and power. As in the 16th and 17th centuries, many new men arrived, most of them not Suffolk-born. Having succeeded in their chosen fields, they (or their sons) had the money to buy themselves into the landowning gentry or aristocracy. John Crowley, who settled in Barking near Needham Market, had inherited England's largest iron-works in Co. Durham; William Churchill, who purchased Dallinghoo, was bookseller, bookbinder and stationer to the king; Samuel Kent, who bought Fornham St Genevieve in 1731, was a wealthy malt distiller from London; and Sir John Holt, who bought Redgrave from the Bacons, was Lord Chief Justice of the King's Bench.

An important group were comprised those who derived wealth from overseas—especially from England's expanding empire. Charles Long, who bought Hurt's Hall at Saxmundham, had inherited the largest property in Jamaica; the Davers family, who took over Rushbrooke, owed their wealth to sugar plantations in Barbados; and Edward Vernon of Orwell Park was a successful naval commander who became a national hero when he captured Porto Bello from the Spanish in 1739.

Although the turnover of estates was very high, life for some old-established families proceeded smoothly enough. In a few cases, their fortunes rose steadily, or even dramatically. The Cornwallises of Brome amassed an impressive record of service to various sovereigns. In different generations they had been appointed steward of the household to Queen Mary, ambassador to Spain for James I, treasurer of the household to Charles II and paymaster-general to George I. Over this long period they naturally accumulated honours: knighthood, baronetcy and earldom. Charles Cornwallis, who lived at Culford, achieved even greater distinction: he was a resourceful army commander (though he lost the battle of Yorktown which sealed the independence of the American colonies): and became governor-general of India. He was created a marquis in 1792.

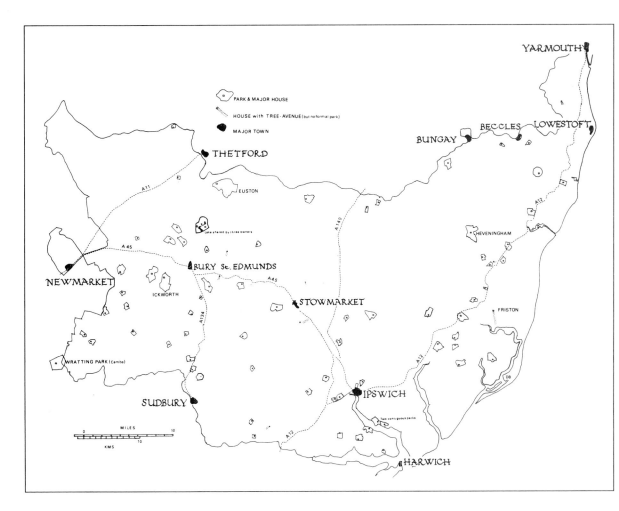

109 *Major houses and parks, 1783: based on Hodskinson's map of Suffolk. Note the paucity of major houses in the north-eastern quarter which was dominated by yeomen, the string of parks close to the modern A12, and the clustering around the social capitals of Ipswich and Bury St Edmunds.*

The progress of the Hervey family is equally fascinating. They had been squires of Ickworth since the 15th century, but had made no great impression until Sir William Hervey was elected MP in 1628. This started a great tradition of parliamentary service which lasted, with one break, until 1906. Sir William raised a regiment for Charles I in the Civil War yet still became sheriff in 1650, and his son John became a favourite of Charles II. It was another John (1665-1751) who suddenly catapulted this family into the ranks of the Whig aristocracy by his shrewd support of the Revolution of 1688 and the Hanoverian succession. In September 1713 he was at Greenwich to welcome the new king, George I, and was created Earl of Bristol for the ensuing coronation.

A minority of county families forged links with the wider world of national government as MPs, courtiers and statesmen. Between 1715 and 1754, about 40 gentlemen resident in the county served as MPs for constituencies in Suffolk and elsewhere. From 1767-70, Augustus Henry Fitzroy, liberal-minded 3rd Duke of Grafton, was Prime Minister (the only time that a man with his principal seat in

Suffolk has held that high office). His tenure, however, was short and unhappy because of his own moral laxity and the attacks of powerful enemies.

The wealthier and more powerful landlords steadily expanded their estates in the 18th century. For example the 2nd and 3rd Dukes of Grafton assiduously acquired land around Euston. In some cases, they embarked on a policy of purchasing individual holdings within a manor, and finally bought out the lord himself. When the land was brought under control, it could be reorganised and improved by re-allotting the parson's glebe, extinguishing commons, enclosing open fields and marling.

Agriculture

Well before 1700, the agriculture of Suffolk was experimental, innovatory and increasingly specialised. Central Suffolk was the first area in England to grow turnips as a field crop. The practice was established by the mid-17th century and provided a means of feeding cattle during winter and spring. Similarly, cabbages were grown on heavy land and fed to beasts which sometimes achieved record sizes. On the lighter land of the south-east, large numbers of carrots were grown, principally to support the growing population of horses. Clover was another popular crop from the mid-17th century onwards. 'Alternate husbandry', whereby certain crops were grown exclusively as fodder for animals, was now normal. This in turn led to new rotations of crops, usually covering four to six years.

In 1718, Edmund Edwards of Levington found that 'crag', a subsoil of sand and shells which can be dug in various places along the east coast, made an excellent natural fertilizer. This discovery gave a new dimension to traditional marling—huge quantities of crag and coprolite were dug and spread during the 18th and 19th centuries, improving the texture of all kinds of land but particularly encouraging the enclosure of sandy heaths in south-east Suffolk.

Although large-scale mechanisation did not affect Suffolk agriculture until the mid-19th century, new pieces of equipment did appear from time to time. Tumble-churns for making butter were in use by 1639 at Fressingfield while a wheel-less swing-plough pulled by only two horses had been developed by 1681. Towards the end of the 18th century, a few wealthy farmers were experimenting with threshing machines and seed drills. Meanwhile, Robert Ransome, in his newly established foundry at Ipswich, was producing a self-sharpening plough-share.

The three major divisions of the Suffolk landscape gave rise to different kinds of farming. To the north-west of Bury a virtually medieval landscape of open-fields, heaths, sheepwalks and rabbit warrens was called the 'Fielding'. In 1764 Kirby described 'delicious champaign fields' still stretching for miles across the Breckland. For centuries this region had relied on two complementary 'crops'—corn and sheep. When the open-fields were fallow they were grazed, dunged and compacted by horned Norfolk sheep who thus contributed to the quality of the next harvest. A similar landscape along the east coast was known as the Sandlings, but it also contained extensive marshland which had been progressively drained since Elizabethan times and used for grazing.

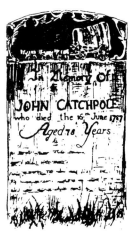

110 *A waggoner's tombstone at Palgrave.*

In the centre of the county, the heavy enclosed land known as the 'Woodlands' or 'High Suffolk' supported a different kind of mixed farming in which dairying was important. According to Arthur Young, the classic dairying area extended from Gislingham in the west to Heveningham in the east, and from Hoxne in the north to Coddenham in the south (illus. 137). The farm of William Dennant of Winston, as described in his inventory of 1702, provides a good example of the complex farming practised here: he grew wheat, barley, oats, peas, flax and hay; he owned 26 dairy cows with five calves and a bull (which together were worth £100), 20 other cattle for fattening, seven horses, 30 sheep, 11 pigs and some poultry; he ground corn with his own horsemill; and he made malt, cheese and butter.

Central Suffolk had been noted for its dairying since at least the 16th century. Its dairy cows were already a distinct regional breed, ancestors of the modern red-polls. In the 18th century, they were then described as small, without horns, and ranging in colour from cream to red. They each cost seven to eight guineas, and were 'the best in all England for giving milk' (illus. 111).

The reputation of Suffolk butter had also been high since Tudor times, and the very best was said to come from the second growth of grass. Some butter was marketed by farmers, particularly at Ipswich Fair, but most was produced by agreement with factors who organised its export to London and elsewhere—chiefly through the port of Woodbridge.

Suffolk had also been capable, as Fuller said, of making 'most excellent cheese', but by the early 18th century the concentration on high-class butter meant that cheese was 'disesteemed'. Indeed, Defoe painted a stark contrast: in

111   *A Suffolk Dun Cow: a long-established local breed famous for producing large quantities of milk. Taken from* Cattle; their Breeds, Management and Diseases *(1852).*

his opinion, Suffolk made 'the best butter and perhaps the worst cheese in England'. Its so-called 'bang' or 'thump' was hard and made of milk which had been skimmed several times, but it kept well and was therefore ideal for use on ships. To some commentators, however, it was only fit for the 'labouring classes' or 'for making wheels for wheelbarrows'.

In coastal marshes and along the valleys of eastern Suffolk, particularly the Waveney, beef cattle were another important specialisation. Many of these beasts were black 'northern' steers. At the age of 14-16 months, they were driven to East Anglia from Scotland and northern England, in the charge of men like 'Peter a Scotch drover' who was buried at Spexhall in 1770. The northern animals were smaller than native cattle, but grew faster on the lush grasses of East Anglia. Halesworth Fair in late October was particularly noted for its 'lean cattle'; after fattening these beasts were again put in the care of drovers and sent to various markets, principally Smithfield in London.

One reason for the progress of agriculture at this period was a new interest in diffusing knowledge. In 1784, de la Rochefoucauld commented, 'It is incredible how intelligent these farmers are, even the smaller ones ... Experiments are made on a big scale by the great landowners and they are promptly taken up by the farmers'. One of the leading influences was Arthur Young, squire of Bradfield Combust, who achieved an international reputation as observer, writer and editor. He had a circle of local friends who discussed agricultural trends and prospects, and welcomed distinguished visitors such as de la Rochefoucauld and Robert Bakewell.

Towns and communications

Commercially and industrially, important changes were taking place in 18th-century Suffolk. Some traditional industries were declining: for example, the weaving and finishing of woollen textiles. Nevertheless, spinning continued to give employment, and woolcombing actually increased—the wool and yarn was sent to weavers in Norwich and Norfolk. Hence in Bury and Ipswich, the feast of St Blaise, patron saint of woolcombers (3 February), was specially celebrated with processions and high jinks.

Of the 98 markets which had been founded in Suffolk during the Middle Ages, only about 25 survived into the 17th century. Travellers often referred to the 'disused' or 'long disused' markets of places like Earl Soham, Stradbroke and Haughley, and the process of weeding-out continued. Of those which existed in the early 1700s, a substantial proportion such as Ixworth and Dunwich were dubbed 'mean', and faded out before the end of the century. On the other hand, some of the larger markets were undoubtedly flourishing and growing in influence. Those of Mildenhall and Beccles were 'plentiful'; Stowmarket was 'well served', especially with corn; and Bungay had 'all manner of Provisions'. Annual fairs survived in greater numbers and were sometimes of real commercial significance. Thus Woolpit was noted for horses and Hoxne for 'Scotch cattle'.

Meanwhile the appearance of successful towns was fast changing. Older timber-framed and jettied buildings, regarded as 'meanly built', were often given new-style Georgian façades in brick or plaster, with parapets, sash-win-

112 *Beccles: houses in Northgate illustrating how older urban property was modernised in the 18th century by adding Georgian façades and parapets.*

113 *Ipswich: the medieval West Gate which stood across St Matthew's Street, demolished 1781-2.*

dows and pedimented doors (illus. 112). Bury St Edmunds has a Georgian appearance, but many timber frames still survive behind its 18th-century façades. Similarly a new air of civic pride led to the improvement of street surfaces and to greater cleanliness. By 1735 Beccles was noted for its well-paved streets, while by 1764 the Thoroughfare at Woodbridge was kept 'so clean that it will tempt the substantial inhabitants to build and reside there'. Medieval walls and gates were now regarded as nuisances to traffic and to health; therefore Ipswich demolished its West and North Gates in 1781 and 1794. The quickening of commercial life, especially in 'thoroughfare towns' like Saxmundham and Newmarket, also meant that local inns were improved as coaching houses and 'places of Good Entertainment'.

As the region's economy became more complex, so individual towns, ports and even villages became identified with particular industries or trades. Woodbridge was noted in the 18th century for the manufacture of fine salt; Aldeburgh was the 'principal place in England for drying fish', particularly sprats; as today, Southwold was associated with brewing because of excellent springs, and with the making of nets; Halesworth dealt with 'great quantities of linen yarn' spun in the neighbourhood; and by the 1730s Woolpit made 'the Best White Bricks'. Meanwhile, Newmarket had become a national centre of horse racing, breeding and training. Twice a year, boisterous crowds enjoyed its races, gambling, cock-fights and plays.

Major changes certainly overtook the two main towns. Since the later 17th century, Ipswich had been in serious economic decline; it built fewer ships, lost its manufacture of cloth and canvas, and saw outside competitors reduce its coal trade. These pressures led to the abandonment 'of the better sort of Houses', and to poverty and unemployment. However, by the mid-18th century, recovery was well under way, even though a new trade with Greenland was only short-lived. More important, though, was the fact that the town shared in the expansion of regional agriculture and became a major centre of the corn trade. So great was the demand for malt that Ipswich could not find enough barley from its own hinterland and had to import it, by coasters, from Norfolk.

Bury changed even more radically. Its traditional industries, such as the weaving of 'Darnex' coverlets, were fast declining and spinning remained as the only significant manufacture. In compensation, however, Bury was becoming a major social capital. It was described by contemporaries as 'The Montpelier of Suffolk and perhaps of England'. The chief trade of the place depended on the nobility and gentry who flocked to it, and on the various commercial and professional services which they demanded. As Defoe put it, 'the beauty of this town consists in the number of gentry who dwell in and near it, the polite conversation among them, the affluence and plenty they live in'. The principal fair held every September on Angel Hill was a great attraction for all classes, not so much for its merchandise as 'for the Company'. Among the entertainments available were assemblies, balls, concerts and plays. Bury got its first purpose-built theatre in the Market Cross in 1734; it was improved by Robert Adam 40 years later. (Interestingly, Ipswich got its first permanent theatre two years later, in 1736, while smaller towns such as Bungay and Sudbury had theatres by the end of the century.) The first newspaper published in the county was *The Suffolk Mercury* or *St Edmundsbury Post* which began in 1714 (to be followed by the *Ipswich Journal* in 1720).

114 *Bury St Edmunds: Market Cross adapted as a theatre in 1734 (Downing's map, 1741).*

Communications had been improving since the 17th century. By 1637, carriers were plying regularly between London and certain Suffolk towns, and after the Restoration, a rudimentary postal system was operating. Five towns in Suffolk were designated major 'stages' and 15 others became minor 'post-towns'. But the general condition of roads remained poor, especially where the land was heavy and full of 'sloughs'. Real improvement did not come until the second half of the 18th century. Under the pressure of increasing traffic, new ideas of road-engineering quickly spread, and the principle of turnpiking was generally accepted (illus. 133).

Turnpike trusts were established by Acts of Parliament. They charged tolls on travellers, so that particular lengths of road could be maintained and improved. Eventually, 14 separate trusts were set up in Suffolk. They administered

115 *Polygonal toll-house at Sicklesmere, on Bury-Sudbury turnpike.*

about 282 miles, mostly the trunk roads of today, and by 1839 were together spending £10,583 a year. This left, however, over 3,000 miles of road under the control of parishes and their highway surveyors. Yet they too were notably improved. Arthur Young, in 1797, wrote that the improvements made to Suffolk's roads in the previous 20 years were 'almost inconceivable'. At the same time many roads, major and minor, were diverted around country houses and parks for the convenience of owners; this is well appreciated today by anyone who drives, for example, through Little Glemham or Culford.

The earliest schemes for improving waterways date back to the 17th century and affected the rivers Lark, Little Ouse and Waveney. By an act of 1705, the Stour was made navigable up to Sudbury; the Blyth was opened to Halesworth in 1761 and the Gipping to Stowmarket in 1793. The cost of the latter project, involving 15 locks, was £26,000 and Stowmarket immediately benefited from increased trade in corn and malt. All the examples mentioned above were 'navigations'—that is, improvements to natural rivers, but true canals were also contemplated. In 1789 alone, proposals were being debated for canals from Stowmarket to Diss, Bishop's Stortford to Lakenheath and Bury St Edmunds to Manningtree.

Religion

Compared with its predecessor, the 18th century is not outstanding for its religious fervour and controversy. The Church of England is often represented as slumbering and neglectful. However, it should not be overlooked that many parishes still repaired their churches and refitted them with, for example, pews, galleries and communion rails. Nor was Suffolk immune from that great wave of religious revival associated with John Wesley. This tireless preacher frequently addressed audiences in Suffolk, usually on his way to and from Norwich. In 1764 at Lowestoft, he had to preach in the open air—'a wilder congregation I have not seen, but the bridle was in their teeth'. He often stayed at Lakenheath, a village with a revivalist tradition going back to the early 18th century. One December evening in 1757, a newly built 'preaching house' there was filled when Wesley preached, and again at five o'clock the next morning.

Population

In the second half of the 18th century, a fundamental change was taking place in Suffolk's population. After a period of decline between 1700 and 1720, the population was again rising and, moreover, continued to rise. Summaries of 472 parish registers from 18th-century Suffolk, published in 1801, show that the numbers of marriages and burials rose slightly whereas the number of baptisms rose considerably, especially in the decades 1750-70 and 1780-90. This widening gap indicated a rising and increasingly youthful population which was to create awesome problems in the early 19th century, particularly in the fields of housing and employment.

8

An Agricultural County in an Industrial Age, 1800-1900

A growing population and rising unemployment were the basic cause of many problems in the 19th century. Suffolk's population increased by over 50 per cent in the first half of the century, passing 335,000 in 1851 and 380,000 by 1901. This increase was despite the large numbers of people leaving the county to settle in other parts of Britain or abroad.

The pauperisation of Suffolk

From 1793 to 1815, with one short break, England was at war with France. This long conflict disrupted the supply of goods from overseas and doubled the price of food. Farmers, therefore, had an excellent opportunity, particularly if they were able to grow corn. Arthur Young commented that 'immense quantities' of pasture were ploughed up in Suffolk, and that some dairy herds were reduced to a tenth of their former size. In the words of one land agent, 'they grew wheat upon land where, in 1792, they never thought of it.'

But already by 1814, the year in which peace celebrations were held prematurely in several parts of Suffolk, corn prices were falling, profits were shrinking and men were being laid off. By 1816-7, the situation was desperate: farmers who had bought land now found that it was not worth as much as they had borrowed, while those who leased land could not pay their rents. The inability of farmers to settle their accounts in turn ruined tradesmen, and farmworkers found it impossible to manage on wages reduced by a third. The combination of reduced demand and increasing population produced, for the first time, a surplus of agricultural labour. A third of Suffolk's working population was unemployed. Contemporary reports speak of gentlemen, formerly 'of comfortable incomes', unable to pay their bills; of farmers, accustomed to dining at inns, walking home to dinner; and the state of the poor as 'lamentable indeed'.

Some indication of the severity of the crisis can be seen by the amounts of money spent on relieving the poor, Suffolk's annual figures always being among the highest in England. The total expenditure of nearly £300,000 in 1817-18 represented over £1 per head of population whereas in Lancashire, by contrast, relief represented only a quarter of that amount. Expenditure continued on a high level, rarely dropping below 75p per head, until the Poor Law Amendment Act was passed in 1834. By that time, half the population of Suffolk was considered to be receiving some form of relief.

The poverty of agricultural workers and their families, by far the largest proportion of the county's population, was to some extent caused by the indus-

116 *Shingle Street: 18 Martello towers were built around Suffolk's coast to resist Napoleon's threatened invasion.*

117 *Assington: the parish workhouse built in 1783 at a cost of £229 15s. 1d. It contained nine rooms, including two for the master. In 1808 the Ward Room contained 18 spinning wheels. After 1834 the building was sold and converted into cottages.*

118 *Tower-mill, Pakenham, built c.1816. This is the only parish in England to have both a working windmill and watermill.*

trialisation of the north of England. For nearly 200 years the women and children of Suffolk labourers had contributed to family income by combing wool and spinning yarn for the Norwich worsted industry, but by the early years of the 19th century the production of yarn was mechanised, and the only work available to most families was on the land. Even a large family with earning children could only just make ends meet, and many had to rely on poor relief. The Crick family of Lavenham are quoted in 1843 as a typical case: their weekly outgoings of 13s. 9d. (rent 1s. 2d., food 11s. 1½d., firing and household necessities 1s. 5½d.) exactly matched the earnings brought in by five workers, including an eight-year-old. And this did not allow for meat, clothing or boots.

The attempt to reduce the costs of relief by incorporating certain Hundreds had failed (allegedly through mismanagement and leniency). Under the Amendment Act of 1834 Suffolk was divided into 18 Poor Law Unions, each having a large central workhouse especially built or adapted for the purpose. These houses, designed to deter rather than attract inmates, gave Spartan accommodation and minimal food, and split families up in separate male, female and juvenile quarters. The new system succeeded in its main aim of reducing the cost of relief—in Suffolk's case by over 40 per cent— but as a result achieved an unenviable reputation. Hatred of the 'spike', as the union workhouses came to be known, continued into modern times, especially in rural areas.

Discontent and violence

Widespread poverty and misery inevitably led to an increase in social unrest. Frequent riots in the second half of the 18th century had been caused by food shortages and, to a lesser extent, by political agitation. They affected towns such as Ipswich, Woodbridge and Sudbury, and also spread into the countryside. In 1815 when the war ended, the smashing of farm machinery at Gosbeck began a new wave of rioting and arson. In various parts of Suffolk, labourers saw threshing machines and mole-ploughs as reducing their chances of employment, particularly during the winter months. Inevitably, too, they were exasperated by the high price of food. The most serious outbreak occurred at Brandon in May 1816, when 1,500 armed men destroyed a butcher's shop and demanded 'bread or blood'. During the next three decades, violence flared up at regular intervals. In the early 1830s, Suffolk experienced the Swing Riots which took their name from an imaginary captain who wrote threatening letters and organised attacks on barns, machinery and workhouses. Despite the imprisonment, transportation and execution of offenders, frequent cases of criminal damage reached a peak when the night skies of Suffolk were lit up by scores of burning ricks and barns. This came after the disappointing failure of Chartism in the years 1838-43. Though Chartist ideas never became deeply rooted in Suffolk, there was enough enthusiasm for 2,000 people to attend a meeting at Debenham and for Friston to be called 'the Suffolk Metropolis of Chartism'.

119 *Mariners Score, Lowestoft: one of the stepped alleys leading from town to beach.*

Housing a growing population

One of the factors adversely affecting the poor was the law of settlement and removal. 'Close' parishes in the control of one or two landowners, restricted the number of labourers taking up residence in order to prevent them 'gaining settlement' and becoming chargeable on the rates. By contrast, 'open' parishes in which there were many landowners, could not control the influx of labouring families. Indeed, whereas the single landowner could ensure that his cottages were of a reasonable standard, open villages and towns were rapidly developed by speculators and jerry builders. In a report of 1850 the 'well built, airy and commodious' cottages on the Bunbury estate at Great Barton were contrasted with 'miserable hovels' in nearby Bury St Edmunds. Many examples of good estate cottages still exist in Suffolk such as those built by the Benyons on the Culford estate and the model houses built by the Tollemaches at Helmingham. The latter were described by Augustus Jessopp as 'the Paradise of the agricultural labourer'.

On the other hand the owners of close parishes could, and did, operate at the expense of their neighbours. By limiting accommodation in their own villages, they forced some of their workers to live in open parishes and walk to work. In about 1850, 97 labourers in the open parish of Great Whelnetham had to walk three or four miles to their work at Rushbrooke, a close parish with few cottages. In this way, places like Huntingfield near Halesworth and Nowton near Bury were able, in the period 1801-51, to hold their population increase down to 10 per cent, whereas the majority of Suffolk parishes experienced a growth of between 40 and 70 per cent.

120 *Helmingham: an outsize monument set up in 1615 to commemorate the lives of four successive Lionel Tollemaches. The family, who originated at Bentley, acquired Helmingham by marriage c.1485 and rebuilt the moated Hall c.1500.*

Generally, Suffolk had a bad reputation for its cottages—'poor and mean', reported Arthur Young. The pressure on housing from the natural growth of population was aggravated by other factors. For example, some owners of 'close' parishes actually demolished cottages to prevent their occupation by 'chargeable' labourers, and no longer did young farmworkers 'live in' with their employers, a fact which surely contributed to the earlier age of marriage. Although figures in the decennial censuses seem to show the numbers of houses keeping pace with the growth of population, this must have been largely through the subdivision of existing houses—a practice which is recorded in Suffolk since at least the early 17th century. New houses were being built, but at a rate slower than the rise of population; indeed, most of the new building took place in the

121 *Somerleyton: part of the estate village built in the 1840s and '50s by Samuel Morton Peto, developer and railway contractor, 'the father of modern Lowestoft'. Carefully designed with varying detail, the houses were far superior to those available in open villages.*

period 1840-60 when the population of most villages had begun to fall. Furthermore, the quality of many new houses and 'rows' was poor. They were run up cheaply and at great speed by 'cottage jobbers', who then let them for maximum rent. Towards the end of the century, Suffolk was said to have 'some of the best cottages in England [no doubt in estate villages] and some of the very worst'.

Town and countryside

In towns, inevitably, conditions were becoming desperately over-crowded. The report of 1850 spoke of 'extreme misery' in Bury St Edmunds, an 'unwholesome and crowded state' in Stowmarket and 'parishes crowded with small houses' in Ipswich. Everywhere the situation was aggravated by workers in nearby close parishes having to find accommodation in the nearest town. Even so, most Suffolk towns experienced a population growth in the first half of the 19th century which was only slightly greater than that of rural parishes. The exceptions were Ipswich, already the largest and most industrialised town in the county, Lowestoft which was fast developing as a fishing port and popular resort, and Brandon, Haverhill and Leiston which attracted immigrants by their various successful industries.

For the only time in English history, the 1851 census showed equal numbers of people living in towns and villages. Thereafter, towns continued to grow at the expense of the countryside. In the second half of the 19th century, almost all Suffolk villages shrank in population whereas Ipswich, Haverhill, Leiston, Newmarket and Stowmarket went on growing, and Lowestoft and the new resort of Felixstowe rocketed to 10 times what they had been when the century began. Villages which did expand were chiefly on the outskirts of growing towns, the outstanding example being Kirkley (later absorbed into Lowestoft) which ended the century with a population 36 times bigger than in 1801!

122 *Ixworth: some of the earliest local authority housing in England. Eight houses were built in 1893 by Thingoe Sanitary Authority, under the Housing of the Working Classes Act of 1890. Victorian Ixworth was notably over-crowded, insanitary and prone to disease. These houses were only built after two enquiries and much local pressure.*

The drift from the countryside had probably begun in the late 18th century, but had been masked by the natural increase of population. The census of 1851 revealed that well over 50,000 people born in Suffolk were already living elsewhere in England and Wales, more than half of them in London. Similarly, nearly half of the inhabitants of Ipswich who were aged 20 or over in 1851 had been born elsewhere in Suffolk.

Countrymen were attracted to towns and industrial districts by the hope of more consistent employment, better pay and a generally more rewarding life. They were actively encouraged to leave by parish officials who hoped to reduce the numbers of paupers 'on the parish'. After the Amendment Act of 1834, the new unions pursued the same policy. Between 1835 and 1837, nearly 2,500 men, women and children were moved from Suffolk villages to 'manufacturing districts', chiefly in Lancashire, Cheshire and Yorkshire. The great exodus continued throughout the century. By 1891, over 23,000 Suffolk-born people were living in the northern counties and over 50,000 were living in London.

The developing colonies, especially Canada and Australia, provided new hope and opportunity. Even before 1834, a constant stream of emigrants left from London and other east-coast ports. In 1832, 793 people left for Canada from Yarmouth alone. After the 1834 act, unions operating through an official agent organised frequent sailings. In May 1836, over 100 men, women and children were brought from north Suffolk by cart and wagon, and embarked for Canada at Wherstead, watched by the guardians of Hoxne Union. Later, in the 1840s and '50s, many left for Australia under government-assisted schemes. For some, the new life brought quick success. In 1852, a labourer from Thelnetham sent home a packet of gold dust to prove his new-found good fortune.

Agricultural Suffolk

The depressed state into which agriculture fell after the Napoleonic Wars continued into the 1850s. Only exceptional farmers could be successful, and then only with the right type of farm and with sufficient capital. J.G. Cooper, who farmed at Blythburgh, was able to boost the low return from his corn crops in 1836 with the income of his flock of 920 sheep.

123 *Portable steam-engine built by Garretts of Leiston 1858.*

During the 19th century, the enclosure of Suffolk, which had begun in the Middle Ages, was completed by parliamentary acts. Between 1770 and 1880, just over one hundred enclosure acts were passed for Suffolk, and most of them before 1840. More than half the acts related to commons, greens and heaths only, mainly in those central districts where most of the farmland had been enclosed generations before. Those acts which did involve open-fields almost wholly concerned parishes on lighter soils, either down the east coast or in the north-west (illus. 137). The only instances of substantial amounts of open-field surviving after 1850 were at Barrow (enclosed in 1853), Withersfield (1854) and Haverhill (1857). Enclosure was certainly not welcomed by all, as we are reminded by Nathaniel Bloomfield's moving poem *Elegy On the Enclosure of Honington Green* (illus. 124), but there can be little doubt that it contributed to agricultural efficiency.

One experiment to improve the agricultural labourer's lot, without recourse to migration, was the Assington co-operative. In 1839, the local squire, John Gurdon, allowed 20 hand-picked labourers jointly to rent 100 acres, and provided them with capital and stock. In just over 10 years, all the capital had been

124 *Honington: the medieval church and cottage (centre) in which the poets Robert and Nathaniel Bloomfield were born. In 1801 the enclosure of Honington Green (foreground) provoked Nathaniel's 'Elegy on the Enclosure of Honington Green':*

In all seasons the Green we lov'd most,
Because on the Green we were free.

repaid and the participants had substantially improved their standard of living. The scheme was extended in 1852 and survived into the 20th century.

Allotments, too, were a boon to hard-pressed labouring families. Begun in the 1820s, they were ably championed, often against the resistance of farmers, by such influential figures as John Henslow, Professor of Botany at Cambridge and rector of Hitcham. By the 1880s, Suffolk had over 15,000 allotments of under one acre, and another 700 of over an acre.

The prospects for farming improved in the 1850s. This was the classic period of so-called 'high-farming', which was to last for a little over 20 years when profits rose in response to demand, and new investment was sunk into buildings, machinery, drainage and other improvements. The dairy farm built about 1870 by the Duke of Hamilton at Easton near Framlingham, now open to the public, is one good example. Not that everyone approved of the prosperity that the period brought: Hindes Groome, who was brought up at Monk Soham, blamed high farming for making 'one huge field' out of five or six earlier fields and for 'swallowing up most of the smaller holdings'— complaints which have a familiar ring today.

The period of high farming finally collapsed with the disastrous harvest of 1879 described locally as 'a summer of cloud and continuous rain'. Corn prices were already falling, as cheap American grain began to flood the English market and undermine the home producer—precisely what farmers had dreaded when the protective Corn Laws were repealed in 1846. So began the 'great depression' which lasted well into the 20th century and hit corn-producing areas like Suffolk particularly badly. Bankruptcies multiplied, the value of land plummeted, tenants became difficult to find, buildings and farms were neglected. The farmworkers, with reduced wages, could only take comfort from the fact that prices had also dropped.

One group able to take advantage of this crisis was of immigrant Scots. Wilson Fox claimed to know of 20 Scots farmers, chiefly from Ayrshire, farming in Suffolk by 1894. They had been attracted by greatly reduced rents (as were their compatriots again in the 1920s) and were recognised as extremely hard working, if ignorant of Suffolk ways. They, and others who weathered the storm, tended to concentrate on the production of milk, beef and pork.

Just before the great depression started, an event occurred which showed the strains within the agricultural community. In 1872, the farm labourers of Exning near Newmarket demanded a wage increase, and were backed by Joseph Arch's newly formed National Agricultural Labourers Union. The employers, having banded into a Defence Association, resisted successive demands and, in the spring of 1874, locked out all the union members. This lock-out spread throughout the eastern counties, but union funds ran out after a few months and the strikers had to capitulate before harvest. The greatly weakened union was finally dissolved in 1896, and no successor appeared until George Edwards founded his Eastern Counties Union in 1906.

125 *Hand-powered threshing machine built by Ransomes in 1844.*

Despite recurrent depressions in agriculture, the 19th century witnessed the mechanisation of farming more than any previous period. Suffolk was well to the fore in this respect. By 1844 the county had about 20 foundries and three

names were already outstanding as producers of first-class agricultural machinery. Garretts of Leiston, which had developed from an 18th-century smithy at Woodbridge, became best known for their steam engines and threshing tackle. Smythes of Peasenhall and Sweffling (and later Ipswich) concentrated on producing drills for seeds, and for seeds and manure combined. Ransomes (best known as Ransomes, Sims and Jefferies) produced a full range of agricultural equipment at their Orwell Works in Ipswich (illus. 126). They developed the first successful steam traction engine in 1842, and collaborated with Fowlers of Leeds to produce the steam ploughing engine in 1856. In 1868 a separate company, Ransomes and Rapier, was formed to handle the production of railway equipment.

126 The Orwell Works, Ipswich: an engraving of 1891 showing Ransomes' 11-acre works. (The adjacent town is omitted!) The complex consisted of smiths' shops, foundries, stores, assembling sheds, timber yards and wharves. The company even provided an 'eating-house' and library.

Despite the inventiveness of these and other firms, their products were adopted only gradually on the land. Dibbles were still used frequently, well after 1850, to make holes into which seeds were 'dropped', very often by children kept away from school. By the 1830s, the sickle had fallen out of general use, only to be replaced on many farms by the scythe, which itself survived well into the 20th century. Yet mechanical reapers were available from the 1850s, incorporating sheaf tiers from the 1880s. Threshing machines, hand-driven at first, were not adopted so early in East Anglia as in the north, but by 1840 horse-driven versions were common, and by the end of the century the steam-driven threshing drum was widely used (illus. 127). Yet the flail, the countryman's 'stick and a half', continued in occasional use, especially for threshing beans, into the 20th century.

Industrial Suffolk

While agriculture remained by far the most important part of Suffolk's economy, many crafts and industries were practised in 19th-century towns and villages. Between 1851 and 1901, about 2,000 men were still employed as blacksmiths and another 1,000 as wheelwrights; in the 1880s maps of the Ordnance Survey

127 *Old Newton: the last set of steam-driven threshing tackle to work regularly in Suffolk, photographed in 1953. Note the belt-drive from traction engine to threshing 'drum', and another to the elevator raising straw on to the stack.*

128 *Garretts' Works, Leiston: a galleried workshop built c.1853 for assembling steam engines. Now restored as a museum.*

showed over 400 windmills still dotted around the countryside. But all these occupations were increasingly vulnerable to outside economic pressures, and sooner or later they decayed as industry became more mechanised, large-scale and centralised in towns. In 1844, 110 places in Suffolk had maltings, so distinctive with their kiln-roofs, yet by the end of the century the number had dwindled to sixty-five. Even more marked, out of about 200 breweries at the beginning of the 19th century, only 40 remained at the end. Today the number is reduced to single figures.

Some completely new industries appeared in the 19th century, often connected with agriculture. The manufacture of artificial fertilisers developed after 1843 when Professor Henslow recognised the potential of coprolites dug in the south-east of the county. The resulting industry, led by such firms as Packard, Prentice and Fisons, soon turned to raw materials imported from abroad. A successful gun-cotton factory was set up in 1866 at Stowmarket and, despite a disastrous explosion in 1871, went on to contribute to the war-effort in 1914-18, while the xylonite factory built at Brantham in 1887 was the first purpose-built plastics factory in the country. Brandon had its own unique industry, the making of gun-flints, which began during the Napoleonic Wars and lingered until well after the Second World War. Beccles and Bungay, by contrast, both developed printing works of national importance.

A artificial manures
B boat/ship building
bl bone lace
br brick
C cocoanut fibre
E engineering/foundry
F fishing
fu fur
G garment making
gc gun cotton
gf gunflints
gl glue making
H horse hair
I printing
K sack making

L leather tanning
M cement
O coprolite digging
P paper making
pl plastics
po pottery
Q quay/wharf
R resort
S straw plait
sa salt
T textiles
W sail cloth
X flax

Burgh Castle **M**

Oulton **E, M**
Beccles **B, E, L, Q**   Lowestoft **B, E, F, R, Q**
Bungay **E, I, P, Q, T**   Kirkley **F**
Barnby **E**   Pakefield **F**
Kessingland **F**

Brandon **fu, gf, Q**

Mildenhall **T, Q**
Barton Mills **Q**
Cavenham **Q**
Fornham All Saints **Q**

Wattisfield **po**
Hoxne **X**   Syleham **T, X**   Halesworth **E, Q, W**
Eye **bl, E, X**   Stradbroke **T**   Southwold **F, sa**
Peasenhall **E**   Walberswick **Q**

Newmarket **E, ra**
Bury St Edmunds **E, L, P**
Woolpit **br**
Debenham **E**   Swefling **E**
Saxmundham **E, L**   Leiston **E**
Stowmarket **A, E, gc, H, K, L, P, Q, T**   Snape **Q**
Combs **L**   Wickham Market **E**
Needham Market **gl**
Witnesham **X**   Melton **E, Q**   Aldeburgh **B, F, Q, R**
Lavenham **C, H, S, T**   Orford **B, F**
Glemsford **C, E, H, T**   Monks Eleigh **L**   Woodbridge **B, E, L, Q**
Clare **S**   Bramford **A**
Haverhill **C, G, H, S, T**   Long Melford **E, C, H, T, X**   Sutton **O**
Sudbury **C, H, S, T, Q**   Ipswich **A, B, E, F, G, I, K, P, Q, T, W**   Alderton **O**
Hadleigh **C, E, L, T**   Newbourn **O**   Bawdsey **O**
Kirton **O**
Bures **L**   Chelmondiston **F, M**   Trimley **O**
Brantham **pl**   Shotley **M**   Felixstowe **O, R**
Nayland **T**

0   5   10 miles
0   6   12 km

129 *Suffolk industries in the 19th century: based on commercial directories. It cannot be assumed that each industry was present throughout the century. Some were very short-lived.*

130 *Drinkstone: a post-mill which contains the date 1689. The whole structure, apart from the round house at the bottom, turns on a large oak post to face the wind. When the mill is in use, the sails are covered with strips of canvas.*

131 *Lowestoft: a view of 1900 showing both the fishing harbour (left) and the pier and beach of the crowded holiday resort.*

132 *Lowestoft: the Low Light built in 1866, dismantled c.1925. The two lights, one on the cliff and the other on the beach, were first established in 1609.*

The coast continued to support its own specialist industries. Ipswich had two shipyards which flourished during the first half of the century but declined after the introduction of iron hulls and steam. In the mid-19th century, however, boat builders still worked at Aldeburgh, Beccles, Lowestoft, Orford and Woodbridge while Southwold continued to refine salt and Woodbridge still had 35 coasting vessels.

It was the fishing boom which most affected the east coast, especially Lowestoft (illus. 131). After the Napoleonic Wars, as Dutch fishing in the North Sea declined, English boats significantly increased their catches. Later, the arrival of railways made it easier to get fresh fish to consumers and encouraged the landing of ever larger quantities of herring and mackerel. The number of local drifters rose from 80 in 1841 to nearly 400 by 1900. They were augmented from the 1890s by an annual invasion of Scots fishermen and fishergirls. Trawling for fish on the sea bottom also developed after 1860. The number of trawlers at Lowestoft grew from eight in 1863 to nearly 300 in the 1880s.

The combing of wool and spinning of yarn, the last major relics of the traditional cloth industry, had almost disappeared during the Napoleonic Wars, and so had the hempen linen weaving in the north and east of the county. To take advantage of the resultant unemployment and local expertise, attempts were made by entrepreneurs to provide new kinds of industry—with varying degrees of success. In the first half of the 19th century, straw-plaiting gave considerable employment for women and children in south-west Suffolk: Lavenham had 300 plaiters in 1851. In the same period, silk mills were built in places as far apart as Haverhill and Bungay, but only really succeeded at Sudbury and Glemsford. (The latter parish made strenuous efforts, in the 1820s, to encourage manufacturers to come and provide employment.) The weaving of horsehair and coconut fibre, introduced in the period 1830-60, became a major industry in the Babergh district and survived until the 1930s. Drabbet, a mixture of linen and cotton from which smocks were made, became the speciality of the Gurteen works at Haverhill, still in existence, and at Syleham on the Waveney.

Communications

Although the industry and commerce of Suffolk had benefited from the improved roads and navigations of the 18th century, the coming of the railways in the 1840s and '50s had an even greater effect. Ipswich and Bury St Edmunds were linked to London in 1846, Lowestoft to Norwich in 1847 and to Ipswich in 1859, and Sudbury to London in 1849. As a result these towns all grew and attracted new industry, especially Ipswich where the new wet dock, also built in the 1840s, allowed modern ships right up to the town. The extension of the

133 *Turnpikes and navigations, 1844: based on J. & C. Walker's map of Suffolk. This shows the main lines of communication just before the railways began to develop.*

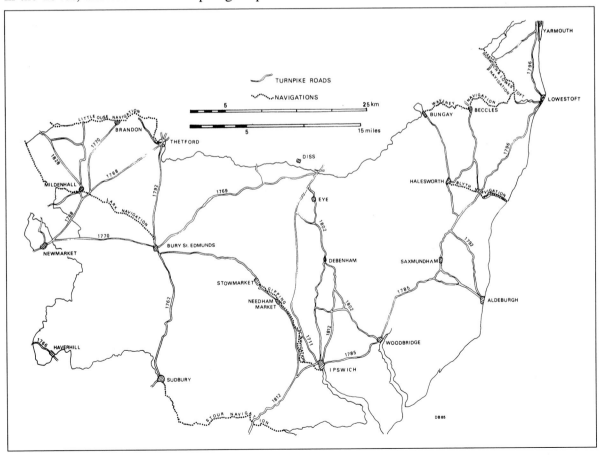

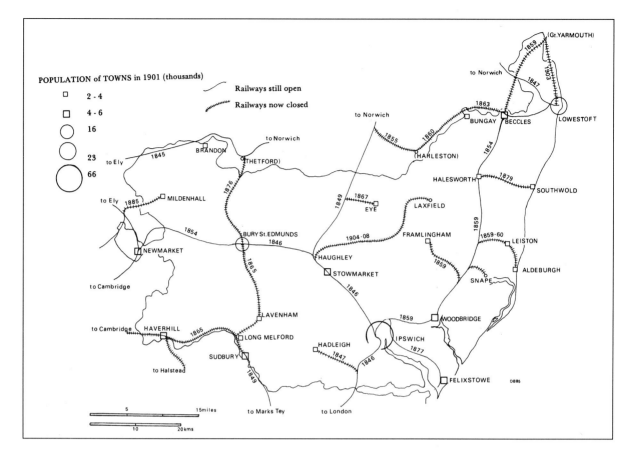

134 *Suffolk towns and railways: the approximate population of each town is given for 1901. The dates on the map refer to the opening of each line.*

railway to seaside resorts—Aldeburgh in 1860, Felixstowe in 1877 and Southwold, by the famous narrow-gauge line, in 1879—brought them appreciably more visitors and trade. On the other hand, railways were a major factor in encouraging people to leave Suffolk: at Orford in 1861, a decrease of population was attributed to 'families in the fishing trade moving with the opening of the railway'. Significantly, the only decade in which the total population of the county actually declined was 1851-61, as the network of major lines was completed.

Religion

One census, that of 1851, attempted to assess the religious state of the country. From it, John Glyde calculated that Suffolk had 895 places of worship: 519 Anglican, 90 Independent, 91 Baptist, 163 Methodist and 31 others. Attending these on the afternoon of Sunday, 30 March 1851 were nearly 133,000 people, 40 per cent of the total population. About 63 per cent of the attenders were Anglican, and the vast majority of the remainder were nonconformist. Of the 163 Methodist congregations in 1851, 84 were Wesleyan and 72 Primitive.

The growth of nonconformity can be crudely measured by the numbers of certificates issued for dissenting places of worship. They show the greatest increase to have been between 1790 and 1840. Although many of these places, well over 1,400 in 50 years, would have been of short duration, in private houses and barns, they do testify to a great upsurge of nonconformity over the whole county. By the end of the century, Suffolk contained over 360 nonconformist meeting places including 162 Methodist, 81 Baptist and 76 Congregational. At the other religious pole, the number of Roman Catholic churches had doubled since 1851 to just over a dozen.

The established Church of England, while it still attracted more worshippers than all the other denominations put together, had inherited many problems and abuses from the past. A report of 1835 showed that the ancient county of Suffolk contained 516 parishes served by 364 incumbents, of whom 152, or nearly half, were pluralists holding more than one living. In 104 parishes the incumbent had no official

135 *St Mary-le-Tower, Ipswich, in 1832: a painting by Samuel Read, showing the interior before the severe restoration of the 1860s. Note the box-pews, stools, galleries and fine organcase. The tall pulpit was in the body of the nave, facing the canopied pew of the two Bailiffs and the Portmen's Aisle.*

house to live in, while a further 90 parsonages were unfit for residence. Of the 449 livings, which included united benefices, 80 were poorly paid curacies and four were donatives depending on the generosity of the patron. The situation had been even worse before 1835, but gradually successive bishops, aided by the Ecclesiastical Commissioners formed in 1836, introduced reforms and the clergy were provided with a higher standard of accommodation.

The greatest influences on the 19th-century Anglican church were the Tractarian or Oxford Movement, which traced its origin to a conference at Hadleigh in 1833, and the less well-known Cambridge Movement. Their search for correct 'order' in worship led to a revived emphasis on choir and altar, and is largely responsible for the general appearance of our church interiors in the 20th century. A large proportion of Suffolk churches underwent a Victorian restoration, varying from modest refurbishing to an almost complete rebuilding as in St Mary le Tower, Ipswich. Only a handful, like the gems at Badley and Brent Eleigh, survived virtually unscathed. The Evangelical movement, too, left its mark, for example in the texts of Bishop Ryle's former churches at Helmingham and Stradbroke.

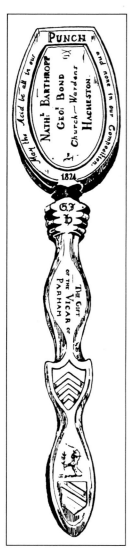

136 *Lemon-squeezer given by vicar of Parham and Hacheston in the hope of healing a rift between his two parishes, 1824.*

Education

Until the establishment of Board Schools after 1870, education was entirely in the hands of voluntary bodies. Prior to the 18th century, the teaching of the basic skills of reading and 'computation' had been left largely to chance, as individual masters and mistresses set up schools, usually in their own houses, wherever there seemed a demand. Only a few places, such as Rougham and Halesworth, had more permanent elementary schools backed by charitable bequests. In the early 18th century, charity schools blossomed under the aegis of the SPCK, and nearly 40 such institutions were set up in Suffolk. Unhappily, few of them survived into the 19th century. With the creation of the British and Foreign School Society in 1808 (which was nonconformist) and the National Society in 1811 (Anglican), many more schools were provided for working-class children. By 1833, 187 places in Suffolk had schools for poor children, attended by over 8,000 pupils—approximately 22 per cent of the child population. After the introduction of government grants in 1833, the number of schools increased steadily, so that by 1870 over 400 schools were open in 374 different places, with accommodation for about 37,500 children, or 60 per cent of the children in Suffolk. After the passing of the Forster Act of 1870, a further 130 voluntary schools were built or rebuilt, together with 80 Board Schools. This raised the total accommodation to nearly 71,000 places, and provided a firm basis for the new century when the Local Education Authorities came into being. The success of this increase can be gauged by estimates of basic literacy. In 1845 just over 50 per cent of Suffolk's population were literate; by 1900 the figure had risen to about 97 per cent.

Parliamentary representation

Before the Reform Act of 1832, Suffolk with its 16 MPs had a ratio of one MP to every 18,500 inhabitants, which was a stronger representation than any of its neighbours—though by no means the best in the country. However, the constituencies were very unequal: the two county members stood for over 250,000 inhabitants, while the 14 borough members represented only 40,000. Furthermore, only a fraction of the people who were theoretically represented had votes.

The 1832 act disfranchised the boroughs of Orford, Dunwich and Aldeburgh which had only 135 votes between them. It also divided the county into two electoral divisions, east and west, each having two members. Between them, these two new divisions had an electorate which by 1844 had risen to about 11,500 voters. The boroughs of Ipswich, Bury St Edmunds and Sudbury continued to send two members each, while Eye was geographically extended to include 10 adjacent villages, but only allowed one MP. In 1832, the total number of Suffolk members was reduced from 16 to 11, and then a few years later to nine. By an act of 1844, Sudbury was disfranchised because of gross electoral corruption.

The second Reform Act of 1867, while it mainly benefited the inhabitants of towns, increased the number of Suffolk's voters from four-and-a-half per cent of the total population to seven-and-a-half per cent. A third act of 1884, by giving the franchise to most working men in rural areas, nearly doubled the

XIII *Onehouse: handsome workhouse built in 1781 for the Incorporated Hundred of Stow.*

XIV *Lavenham: medieval house in Prentice Street. By the 19th century converted into three small tenements to accommodate working families.*

XV *South Cove: drying-shed of a small business making hand-made bricks. A traditional industry surviving into the late 20th century.*

XVI *Kersey: former industrial complex of watermill, miller's house and maltings.*

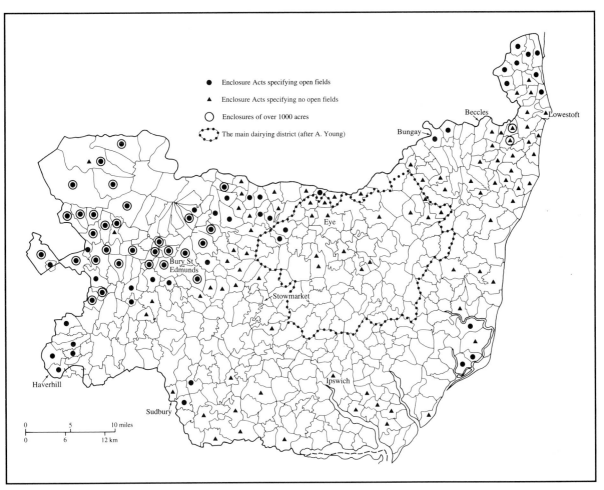

137 *Parliamentary Enclosure, 1720-1860: only the west and extreme north-east of Suffolk had large areas of unenclosed land in the form of open-fields, commons and marshes. Over most of the county, enclosure had taken place much earlier and left relatively small areas, mainly commons and road verges, to be 'improved' by parliamentary acts.*

nation's electorate to five millions. It also re-arranged the electoral pattern of Suffolk into five divisions based on the towns of Lowestoft, Eye, Stowmarket, Woodbridge and Sudbury. Ipswich and Bury St Edmunds retained their status as parliamentary boroughs, though the latter was reduced to a single member.

Although their outcome was usually predictable, and they were often un-contested, elections in the 19th century could be very lively and colourful. An early example was that of 1820 in Ipswich, an extremely close-fought and corrupt contest. Freemen from all over England were paid to come and vote, regardless of expense. Many whose votes had been bought were 'cooped' in country inns, until the time came for them to be transported into Ipswich and to vote under surveillance. After petition and counter-petition, the two Whig candidates were declared the winners—even though one of the Tories had already been triumphantly 'chaired'.

138 *Edward Fitzgerald of Bredfield and Boulge (1809-83), re-creator of 'Rubaiyat of Omar Khayyam'.*

Another exciting election came in 1885, when many of the agricultural workers of Suffolk voted for the first time. The men of Glemsford, a Liberal stronghold where the mat-makers had been on strike earlier that year, were required to vote three miles away at Long Melford. Encouraged by speeches from Joseph Arch, they organised a march to the poll with flags, banners, the regalia of friendly societies and a band. In Melford, however, the carnival atmosphere gave way to frustrating delays, arguments and stone-throwing. By the end of the day, groups of men, well lubricated with beer, were roaming the streets, smashing hundreds of windows and wrecking public houses. Eventually, in order to clear the streets, the magistrates had to call in troops and read the Riot Act.

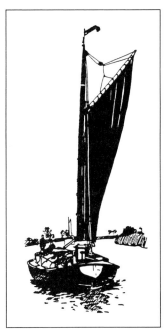

139 *The* Albion, *last of the freight-carrying wherries of the Norfolk and Suffolk Broads.*

9

Stagnation and Revival: the 20th Century

For Suffolk the 20th century has been full of change and drama, yet its study has barely begun. This chapter can only tentatively survey the main trends, and it is hoped that others will soon substantiate, or modify, these findings with more detailed work.

In the years 1900-39, the population of Suffolk grew by 8.5 per cent to 402,200. This increase was small by national standards, and conceals the fact that it was only major towns and dormitory villages which were actually growing, Ipswich with its industries of engineering, brewing and malting continued to attract immigrants as it had done in the 19th century: from 1901 to 1931 its population grew by 31.3 per cent to make it by far the largest town in the county with 87,502 inhabitants. Lowestoft as an industrial centre and holiday resort attracted many new residents, and in the same three decades increased its population by 40 per cent to 41,769. However, the place which showed the fastest growth was the new resort and port of Felixstowe, 'the Queen of the East Coast'. Its population escalated by 443.6 per cent, from 2,720 in 1901 to 12,067 in 1931. Meanwhile most rural areas, including many of the smaller market towns, continued to decline.

140 *The narrow-gauge Southwold Railway, 1879-1929: Halesworth station.*

After 1879, the exodus from rural areas was fuelled by prolonged agricultural depression, and lasted generally until the 1930s. For example, Lawshall from 1841 to 1931 lost 35.4 per cent of its population while Worlingworth lost 39 per cent. In 1901, the RDC of Hoxne lamented the loss of a quarter of its population in only 40 years. As late as 1931, 33 of Suffolk's 37 census areas still showed that migration was 'outward on balance'. Of course, exceptions to these general trends can be found. Better housing in estate villages, such as in Helmingham, ensured a slower rate of depopulation. Occasionally, a successful local industry or institution enabled a village to remain stable or even grow. Thus, Brantham profited from its xylonite works established in 1887, and Martlesham grew between the wars because of its 'Aeroplane Experimental Establishment'.

Economically, the life of Suffolk in the early 20th century was dominated by agricultural depression, caused by the unrestricted importation of cheap food from abroad. In 1902, having interviewed many local landowners, farmers and agents, Rider Haggard described conditions as 'disastrous'. Agricultural prices were low, the value of land was declining, rents had fallen by a half or even two-thirds, wages were rising, and the farming community constantly complained of the burden of taxes, rates and tithes. As a result, some land was allowed to grass over, buildings were neglected, less money was invested, the

115

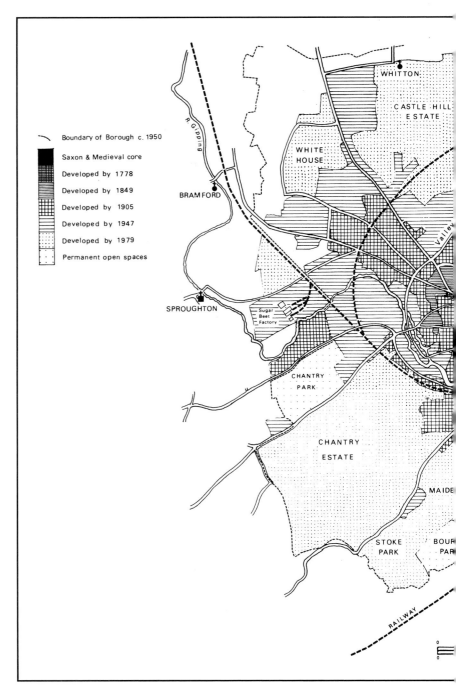

141 *The growth of Ipswich: although the town developed suburbs from at least medieval times, its expansion in the 19th century was unprecedented in scale, and has continued apace in this century. Note that Victorian growth left an 'island' around two large houses (X), which was not developed until the early 20th century.*

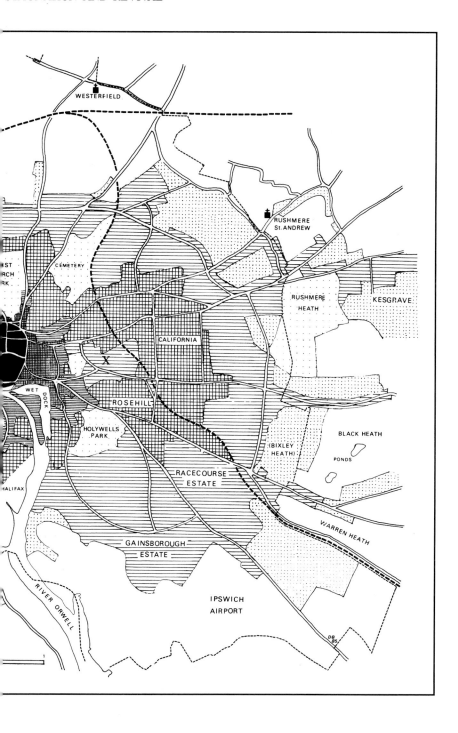

142 *Felixstowe: the largest container-port in the U.K., with regular sailings to most parts of the world. The original basin (in distance) was created by Col. Tomline in 1886, but development has been particularly rapid since 1951. The port has recently been extended northwards into an 'area of outstanding natural beauty'.*

number of agricultural jobs declined, and bankruptcies mounted among farmers. Conditions on heavy clay land were bad because drainage and other costs were high, while much of the sandy land was 'given up to sport'. Yet it is important to note that, by hard work and specialisation, some enterprising farmers weathered the storm quite well. Oliver Johnson of Barrow, chairman of West Suffolk County Council for 15 years, produced vegetables, eggs and poultry for the London market, and Clement Smith of Trimley built a small factory which made cheddar cheese.

During the First World War, Britain had to produce more of its own food, and the farming industry gratefully responded. By 1920, agricultural prices were 192 per cent higher than they had been in 1913. Land under grass was again ploughed, with the help of steam-ploughs and the new-fangled tractor. Many farmers bought land during or just after the war, when large numbers of estates were broken up as a result of death duties and rising costs. Unfortunately, this revival was short-lived. The Corn Production Act of 1917 which

143 *Culpho: ploughing heavy land with a single-furrow plough drawn by two Suffolk Punches, c.1908.*

guaranteed minimum prices and wages was repealed in 1921 and, once again, the farming industry was thrown back into depression. Prices fell rapidly: by 1931 they were only 12 per cent above pre-war levels. Farms on heavy land were again falling derelict because no spare money could be found for drainage, phosphates or lime. Some of the lighter land with its low yields was not worth ploughing and reverted to 'gorse, bracken and rabbits'. George Pretyman of Orwell Park abandoned nearly 1,000 acres which had been cropped during the war, while the newly established Forestry Commission bought huge areas in the Breckland for a few shillings an acre.

The renewed depression of 1921-39 was not, however, so deep as that prior to 1914. Although some land reverted to pasture, about 70 per cent of Suffolk's farmland remained arable. Once again, certain individuals survived well enough. Justin Brooke built up a large holding at Wickhambrook producing, among other things, rose trees and fruit juices. The Elveden estate even managed to make the Breckland productive, by combining cattle with the growing of lucerne as a fodder crop. What ensured a brighter future for the farmer, however, was that central government slowly accepted the need to protect British agriculture. Sugar beet was subsidised, and the marketing of agricultural produce was improved by setting up special boards. Farmers invested more in machinery such as tractors and lorries, and showed a new interest in the rearing of pigs and poultry. The poultry population of Suffolk rose from one-half million in 1930 to two million in 1935. Collectively these developments did not make farming prosperous but they saved it from ruin and laid the foundations for rapid development during the Second World War.

For centuries, the payment of tithe had caused friction between the farming community and the Church of England. In the 1930s, this irritation erupted into the so-called Tithe War. When agriculture had slumped again in 1922, many of the new owner-occupiers felt the burden of tithe for the first time. Arrears piled up and defaulters were brought to court. Two monuments, at Wortham and Elmsett, record how bailiffs were sent to distrain on the goods of local farmers. A National Tithepayers' Association was formed in 1930 and kept up a lively campaign until the Second World War. The first president was a Suffolk farmer, Albert Mobbs of Oulton. Some of the protesters were nonconformist but all objected to the injustice of making one economic group support a church which certainly did not represent the whole population. Thanks to their efforts, the payment of tithe has now disappeared.

Village life

In 1900, Suffolk was still a deeply rural county. Only five towns had more than 5,000 inhabitants and their population amounted to only 35 per cent of the total. The majority still lived in more than 500 villages and small market towns. Unfortunately for them, rural life in the early 20th century was at a low ebb: farming was barely profitable and its workforce was shrinking, shops were closing, craftsmen like wheel-wrights and millers were giving up their trades, while the rural population as a whole was declining and ageing. For agricultural labourers, the outlook was particularly bleak. Their housing was poor, their diet monotonous. Improved wages won in the 1880s and '90s were offset by rising prices after 1900. Their work was hard and repetitive, and gave few chances of promotion. Furthermore, villages still had social hierarchies in which the principal farmers, clergy and landowners usually kept control.

The demoralisation of country-dwellers was made worse by their increasing awareness of the outside world. Since the introduction of compulsory education in 1880, most countrymen were literate enough to read newspapers, now comparatively cheap to buy, and had some smattering of geography and current affairs. The bicycle, too, gave ordinary people a new mobility and taste for exploration, while the railway system afforded easy opportunities for travelling further afield. The 'bright lights' and superior amenities of towns, whether Ipswich down the road, Manchester in the north or the ever-seductive London, were a perpetual lure for the young, dissatisfied and ambitious. On top of this came the appeal of emigration to the new worlds of America, Canada, Australia and New Zealand.

144 *Debenham: the Foresters' Hall, erected in 1905 to seat 600.*

145 *Medieval industrial methods lingering into modern times: Mrs. Fenetta Clarke weaving silk on a hand-loom at her home in Pump Lane, Glemsford, c.1900. She is mentioned in the 1881 census as 'silk weaver'.*

Yet, paradoxically, this period witnessed enormous efforts to make village life more varied and satisfying. As well as Friendly Societies and clothing, coal and pig clubs inherited from the 19th century, many new institutions and events were established: social gatherings such as Penny Readings, lantern and film shows, whist drives, dances and outings by train or charabanc; educational facilities such as night schools, parish libraries and reading rooms; recreational clubs for football, cricket or quoits; for the other half of the population, Mothers' Meetings, Girls' Clubs and the Women's Institutes. The new custom of producing parish magazines is particularly important for today's local historian. When written by an observant and public-spirited clergyman, this could virtually be a parish newspaper covering all aspects of ecclesiastical and secular life. All these various initiatives did not halt the decline of rural areas, but they certainly improved the lot of those who remained.

The First World War

In 1914, men flocked to the colours with patriotic enthusiasm. A single meeting at Southwold in September 1914 produced 60 recruits who were sent off with bands and crowds. Like other regiments, the Suffolks were rapidly expanded from two to 27 battalions. Thousands of young men left, many to be killed and even more to be wounded or maimed. The 7th Battalion was almost completely wiped out at Cambrai in 1917. At Carlton Colville in 1918 Canon Bignold wrote of a family which had lost all three of its sons, and of a man who had been wounded three times yet survived. By the end of the war, this community of about 3,000 souls had lost 90 men in the army or navy and another 37 fishermen on patrolling and minesweeping duties—a total of 127 men. War memorials all over the county tell of similar losses and sacrifice.

Meanwhile, the civilian population of Suffolk were blacking-out their homes and experiencing the first air raids. Southwold was bombed by Zeppelins in August 1916, and Felixstowe was attacked in 1917 by German seaplanes. In April 1916 German ships bombarded Lowestoft with about 60 shells; some 40 houses were destroyed and four lives lost. But much more important was the dramatic way in which ordinary life was disrupted and transformed.

To meet the threat of invasion, men who were exempt from military service were enlisted into the Volunteers and National Guard, and women were increasingly diverted to war work and farming. Incessant military traffic was seen on local roads and railways; troops were billeted in private houses; horses were picketed on local commons; summer-time was introduced in 1917 to help the war effort; and 'spy-mania' became a common obsession. As food became scarcer, prices escalated and great efforts were made to plough and dig more land. In December 1917, rationing was introduced and coupons were issued for sugar, meat, butter and margarine. Finally, nobody could forget the carnage on the Western Front because the rumble and thud of the guns were often heard in many parts of Suffolk.

Canon Bignold's record of life at Carlton Colville brilliantly evokes the horrifying crisis of 1918 when the Germans were still able to mount a mighty offensive. One Suffolk battalion was reduced to 47 men but in three days was restored to 900 by new drafts. To replace the huge losses, men up to the age of 50 were called up. As the battle swayed to and fro, Bignold wrote movingly of 'this crucifixion of humanity'. At home, he described the strenuous efforts to grow more food, promote savings and still prepare for the strong possibility of enemy raids or even invasion. The Canon also appreciated that profound social changes were taking place. The wages of labourers had doubled; social distinctions were being dropped; and the outlook of ordinary village lads was transformed by the experience of travelling to France, Greece or Palestine. Finally, he instinctively knew the enormity of the world events he was witnessing, especially the collapse of the German and Russian empires and the advent of Bolshevism— events 'comparable only to the fall of the holy Roman Empire'.

A new style of government

No account of life in the 20th century can ignore the work of county councils created in 1888, or of district and parish councils established in 1894. Though the records of these bodies are copious, they are as yet almost unused.

Suffolk had been traditionally administered by magistrates meeting in Quarter Sessions, one court for the east and another for the west. The old system was already a complicated blend of justice and administration with a structure of committees, sub-committees and paid officers. Magistrates met regularly, issued by-laws, licences and orders, and often took on new responsibilities delegated by acts of parliament. The main significance of the Local Government Act of 1888 is that it took county administration from the hands of appointed magistrates and gave it to elected councillors.

A fascinating controversy in the 1880s had questioned the wisdom of having two divisions of magistrates for east and west Suffolk. In 1882, a letter signed by 89 magistrates argued for one Quarter Session for the whole county, meeting at Ipswich. The western court objected to the proposal and appealed to the Marquis of Bristol as hereditary High Steward of the Liberty of Bury St Edmunds. These disagreements were overtaken by the Local Government Bill which proposed a single county council for Suffolk. The magistrates and ratepayers of the west immediately leapt to defend the principle of 'Home Rule'. In the Commons Lord Francis Hervey put forward an amendment seeking two administrative counties, but it was narrowly defeated. When the bill got to the Lords, the Marquis of Bristol argued the west's case vigorously, and won the support of the Prime Minister, Lord Salisbury. As a result, the amendment was carried decisively by 122 votes to 68, and West Suffolk retained its ancient independence for nearly another century.

At first the responsibilities of the new county councils resembled those of the old Quarter Sessions. They took over the administration of main roads and bridges, shared the running of the police forces with local magistrates, and carried out less costly functions such as the regulation of weights and measures, control of animal diseases and inspection of food and drugs. Their initial costs were surprisingly low: in their first year West Suffolk spent only £16,207 and East Suffolk £30,500. Relentlessly, however, the budgets grew as both county councils expanded their services and took on new responsibilities (illus. 147).

146 *Great Finborough: village signs symbolise new attitudes to rural life.*

A major milestone was the Education Act of 1902, which gave county councils the status of local education authorities and greatly increased their work. By 1910, East Suffolk was spending over £230,000 and education alone counted for nearly half. Other new services included the registering of midwives, administration of smallholdings and licensing of vehicles. In 30 years, West Suffolk built up an estate of over 10,000 acres which was, in 1939, rented to 579 smallholders.

After the First World War, East Suffolk achieved distinction in two fields. First, they established a new system of secondary or 'area' schools which, with new buildings and playing fields, 'attracted visitors from all over the world'. Secondly, they were amongst the earliest authorities to realise the importance of planning; after a conference in 1931, they set up a central planning department with a Planning Officer, six area planning committees and an advisory panel of experts.

Another important milestone was the Local Government Act of 1929. This made county councils responsible for all roads in rural districts and, by abolishing the Poor Law Unions, for the running of workhouses and granting of assistance to people in their own homes. Accordingly, the total expenditure of East Suffolk jumped from £554,500 in 1929 to £873,000 in 1931.

In the early days of county councils, elections were usually quiet and predictable though occasionally, especially in large open villages like Rattlesden,
Hitcham and Bildeston, a vigorous contest took place along party lines. At Bury
in 1889, 16 candidates stood for six places, an event 'unprecedented in the
history of the borough'. In general the traditional leaders of local society retained
the authority they had held in the past. In the first elections of 1889, 60 of the
105 councillors in the two councils were returned unopposed, 53 were magistrates as well, nine were clergy, seven were titled, seven had military ranks, and
at least 26 were farmers. Nevertheless, the 'feudal' interest was already weak-
ening because at least 24 councillors were local businessmen or industrialists,
and eight others were professionals such as solicitors. Added to this, there was
the occasional working-class representative like S.W. Downes of Glemsford
who was a blacksmith and loom-maker.

By 1939 the picture had naturally changed. The clergy were less prominent,
the military contingent was stronger (especially in West Suffolk) and 14 women
had been elected. Returns for East Suffolk in 1967 show a much greater diversity among 66 elected councillors: farmers were still the largest occupational
group (19), 10 had military ranks, 13 described themselves as retired, and nine
were women. The commercial, industrial and professional occupations ranged
from a signal lampman and electrical fitter to doctor and company director. The
changing social backgrounds, occupations and political leanings of local

Total Expenditure of East and West Suffolk County Councils

Date	East	West
	£	£
1889-1890	30,565	16,207
1899-1900	83,184	65,860
1909-1910	230,093	166,099
1917-1918 ⎫	No records	198,081
1918-1919 ⎬	1915-20	322,774
1919-1920 ⎭		483,767
1929-1930	660,001	503,242
1931-1932	——	755,065
1939-1940	1,098,623	597,343
1949-1950	2,560,834	1,265,462
1959-1960	5,345,280	3,075,299
1969-1970	13,867,474	8,478,366*
1972-1973	21,071,908	14,060,393

Amalgamation in 1974

1983-1984	£240,386,000

* £ devalued 1967—inflation 6.6%

147 *Total expenditure of
East and West Suffolk
County Councils: as
separate bodies from
1889 to 1973, and after
amalgamation in 1974.*

councillors, from 1888 to the present day, is a fascinating subject which needs much more detailed investigation.

District councils, founded by the Local Government Act of 1894, were modelled on earlier bodies called Sanitary Districts. Their principal task, whether urban or rural, was to look after basic services such as water supply, sewage disposal and public health. Urban districts usually had more income and took on extra responsibilities like highways, street lighting and cemeteries. As a result of the 1894 act, Suffolk was divided into 18 rural districts and eight urban districts. By 1935, the pattern had been changed to 14 rural and 11 urban districts.

148 *Doric Cinema, Newmarket, opened in 1939: over 50 'dream palaces' were built in Suffolk.*

Perhaps the most important achievement of these bodies is the building of council houses after the First World War. They improved accommodation for those who had wholly depended on rented or 'tied' houses, often seriously sub-standard. By 1920, schemes for 1,268 homes had been started in East Suffolk, and for 473 houses in the west. The authority which achieved most in this field was Ipswich; between the wars the borough built 4,200 council houses, mainly on the northern and south-eastern fringes of the town. At the same time it demolished over 2,000 'slums' (which today would probably be classed as 'conservation areas') .

For centuries the secular and ecclesiastical affairs of each parish were regulated by its vestry. In 1894 this was replaced by the parish council, which was greeted enthusiastically as a means of breaking the hold of 'squires, parsons and farmers'. In the early years, many parishes did, indeed, produce large numbers of candidates and voters. In 1894, Gazeley had 13 candidates for seven seats; at Bacton 103 out of 115 qualified electors went to the poll; at Great Ashfield, crowds waited to hear the results declared 'amid considerable excitement'. Although the farming interest normally won, parishes were sometimes riven by controversy. It was claimed that labourers in the Stowmarket area were intimidated by a radical clique, and that Old Newton had been subjected to 'venemous attempts to set class against class'. Generally, the political enthusiasm died down after 1900, when it was realised that parish councils 'could not work miracles'. Nevertheless, in spite of the very limited powers given to them, these councils remained useful sounding-boards of local opinion and controversy. At Bardwell, for example, arguments about local charities and the village school were exacerbated by rivalry between Anglicans and Baptists.

The Second World War

In the years 1939-45, the life of Suffolk was again galvanised by war. The county regiment was once more expanded, and the old yeomanry converted into artillery units. Suffolk battalions fought in many areas of conflict, at Dunkirk, at the fall of Singapore, in Burma and in Normandy on D-Day. Enemy aircraft bombed Suffolk on many occasions, and several actions took place off its coast in 'E-boat alley'. One of the earliest tragedies of the war was the sinking of HMS *Gypsy* which hit a mine in the mouth of the Orwell; nearly all her crew were drowned.

The greater emphasis on air-power probably had the most lasting effects on Suffolk. The first bombing attack against Germany was mounted from Wattisham,

149 *The towers, 360 feet high, of radar station built 1937 at Bawdsey, where pioneering research had been done. A vital system in the Battle of Britain.*

and before the war was over the county was dotted with no fewer than 34 airfields. Most of them were created by bulldozing the flatter parts of Suffolk's hedged landscape—an omen of major changes to come. They were used by the British and American Air Forces, especially for the great bombing offensive against Germany and occupied Europe. From the airfield of Framlingham, for instance, the 390th Bombardment Group of the 8th American Air Force flew 300 missions against the enemy and dropped 19,000 tons of bombs; 176 young men from that base died on active service.

Basic amenities

At the end of the Second World War, Suffolk was poorly provided with modern amenities, particularly in rural areas. For their water, most countrymen still depended on wells, springs and 'tea-ponds', which might easily dry up during summer droughts. Sewerage hardly existed outside the towns, and electricity had not penetrated far. In 1946, the Planning Officer of West Suffolk described conditions as 'frankly disgraceful' and promised rapid improvements. By 1962, RDCs in the west were able to report that water was piped to all major settlements and that 44 parishes had been sewered.

Post-war censuses show the progress of this great revolution in living standards. In 1951, out of 132,456 households in Suffolk, 34 per cent were entirely without WCs and many others shared, 53 per cent without fixed baths and 28 per cent without piped water. Twenty years later, out of 185,175 households, only 11 per cent lacked baths and 4 per cent were without WCs. By then piped water was generally available, and only 11 per cent of households did not have *hot* water.

150 *Outside lavatory, two seater for adults and children. A normal facility until the 1950s.*

Natives and newcomers

After the Second World War, the local population began to grow again strongly. Indeed, in the decade 1961-71, the population of Suffolk rose by no less than 15.2 per cent, making it one of the fastest growing parts of the British Isles. Over 70 per cent of the increase was the result of inward migration stimulated by planning policies.

For several generations the west had been the more rural and feudal half of the county, and its population had actually declined between the wars. In 1961, the county council decided to attract 40,000 new residents to inject new life into the region, an increase of more than a third. The towns of Haverhill and Bury St Edmunds were to grow by 10,000 each, with smaller expansions at Sudbury, Mildenhall, Brandon, Newmarket and Hadleigh. Large new estates of council housing were built, while new firms and industries were deliberately attracted to give more employment. By the mid-1960s about 120 new factories had been built and about 1,600 new jobs in manufacturing industry were being created each year.

This planned migration stimulated an even greater degree of voluntary migration. A wave of private building swept over local towns and many villages. In the mid-1960s, over 2,000 new houses were erected in West Suffolk each year; most of them in private estates. In addition, many traditional buildings were restored. In the years 1967-76, West Suffolk County Council gave 19,100

151 *Former railway station at Marlesford, on an abandoned branch-line to Framlingham. Ironically, this relic of Victorian enterprise lies beside the busy A12.*

grants for conversions and repairs. Many of the newcomers were commuters who lived in villages and worked in towns. They and other migrants were attracted by improving opportunities for employment, rising affluence, houses which were comparatively cheap and the general attractiveness of a hitherto undeveloped region.

Meanwhile, East Suffolk followed a more cautious policy, and its key areas grew less strongly. While in the decade 1961-71 the district later known as St Edmundsbury grew by 28.7 per cent and Babergh by a huge 34.6 per cent, Ipswich grew by only five per cent and Suffolk Coastal District by 7.6 per cent. Nevertheless, a new government strategy for south-eastern England proposed, in 1966, to expand the population of Ipswich by a staggering 70,000 in 15 years. The plan envisaged a string of new developments up the Gipping valley, increasing Needham Market alone from 1,800 to about 20,000 people.

The unprecedented growth and breathtaking visions of the 1960s were not, in fact, sustained. After 1970 the emphasis changed nationally to the building of new towns, and it became more difficult to attract new industry to Suffolk. The climate of local opinion was changing as well, and planners were beginning to use new terms such as 'limited growth' and 'planning restraint'. By 1979, the county councils had designated about 90 'conservation areas' and 23 places of outstanding historical importance, while they accepted the Stour valley, Orwell estuary and Sandlings as areas of outstanding natural beauty. In spite of this slowing of development, however, the county still grew by 8.4 per cent in 1971-81, as compared with a figure of 0.3 per cent for England as a whole.

The growth of Suffolk since the war conceals many local variations. Planning authorities encouraged large 'key' villages like Elmswell and Capel St Mary to grow very fast; as a result, their historical cores were clamped, incongruously,

152 *Spexhall 'Hut' re-erected after military use, typical focus of village life from the 1920s.*

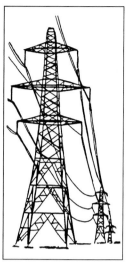

153 *Thornham Magna: modern pylons striding across central Suffolk.*

with estates of suburban-style housing. Many other villages, however, usually with smaller than average populations, remained fairly stable or continued to shrink. Thelnetham and Dallinghoo have experienced no dramatic change in population for many decades, and Cookley and Benacre are steadily declining.

Indeed, much debate in recent years has centred on so-called 'dying' villages. Some are small, remote and predominantly agricultural settlements where major development is discouraged and the prospects for employment are not good; in such places, empty cottages often fall into the hands of weekenders, and the number of amenities tends to shrink. Sudbourne declined from a population of 631 in 1831 to 298 in 1981, and since the war has lost its shops, post-office and school. Ampton is in danger of dying altogether: from 1971-81 its population fell by 50 per cent to 33, yet it had 147 inhabitants in 1841. The decline of rural bus services also means that 30 per cent of Suffolk households who have no car are increasingly at a disadvantage. In 1985, the north-east of Suffolk, which has many of these stagnant and declining parishes, was designated a Rural Development Area in the hope of revitalising social and economic life.

Another kind of 'dying', or rather 'ageing', community is the especially attractive conserved village. As the old agricultural and native population breaks up, such places are increasingly colonised by middle-class newcomers—particularly the retired. One such village in the south of the county has already been described, rather disrespectfully, as 'God's waiting room'. The census of 1981 revealed that 25.4 per cent of Suffolk's population were of pensionable age, as compared with only 22.6 per cent under the age of 15—a dramatic turn-around since the early 19th century.

154 *The population of Suffolk, 1801-1981: the county's population rose steadily, in spite of massive migration to other parts of Britain and abroad. In fact, it was major towns which mainly grew while rural areas generally declined. Only in the last generation has the rural population recovered.*

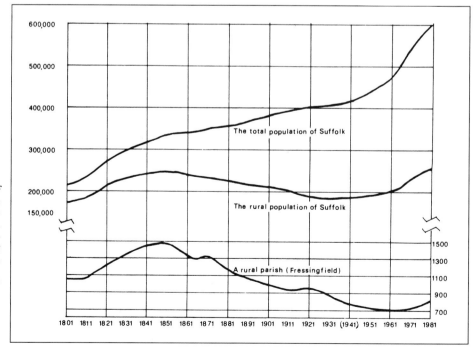

The economy of the county has also changed fundamentally. In 1961 the farming community was still the largest economic group but by 1981 they were outweighed by those in retail trade, in transport, engineering and various professional or technical services. By the 1980s, Suffolk was firmly part of the industrialised and technological world with industrial estates, ever-changing patterns of retail trade and rapidly expanding service industries. The improved A45 (now A14), Orwell Bridge and thriving Haven ports demonstrate Suffolk's importance as a gateway to Europe.

155 (left) *The Orwell Bridge: opened in 1982, 'one of the largest continuous structures in the world', allows the traffic from the London area and the industrial Midlands to by-pass Ipswich on the way to Felixstowe. The graceful super-structure is carried on 19 piers, which rest on piles going 131 feet into the ground.*

156 (below) *Sizewell in 1985: the nuclear power station, with gas-cooled reactor, built in the early 1960s at a cost of £60 million. The proposal to build a second station, using a pressurised water reactor, provoked the longest-running enquiry in English planning history (January 1983 to March 1985).*

157 *Combine harvesting in 1974—a Dania 1600 at work.*

A new agricultural revolution

Since 1939, the farming industry of Suffolk has flourished by combining the enterprise of farmers with strong protectionism from the state and taxpayer. Incomes and profit margins rose dramatically, especially in the 1970s, and large farmers were particularly well placed to benefit from higher output, guaranteed prices and grants. Between 1955 and 1979, the total number of farms and smallholdings in Suffolk was halved from 8,067 to 3,977, while the total acreage of large farms (over 500 acres) almost doubled. The revival of the industry precipitated yet another Agricultural Revolution, more radical than its counterpart in the 17th and 18th centuries and with far-reaching consequences economically, environmentally and socially.

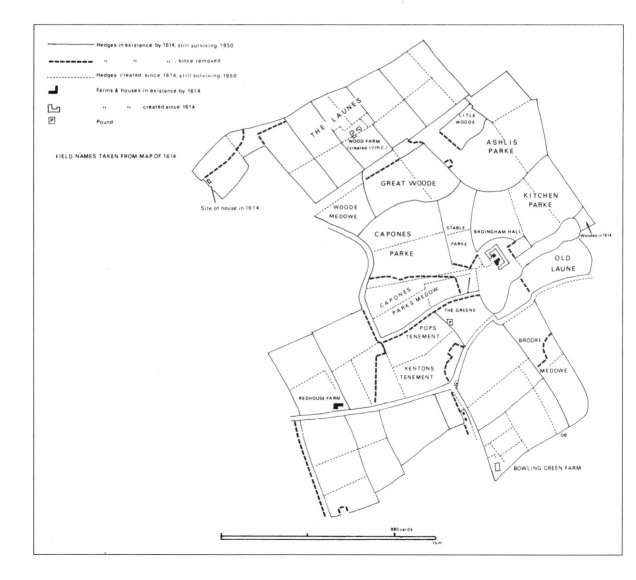

The swing towards arable farming, which began in the late 18th century, has continued so that 83 per cent of available land is now ploughed and all forms of grassland account for only 12 per cent. Simultaneously, the industry mechanised itself as never before. The number of combine harvesters rose from a mere 32 in 1942 to 2,970 in 1968. Traditional implements were greatly improved, and completely new machines introduced such as beet harvesters, sprayers and rotary balers. Inevitably the population of working horses plummeted from 44,000 in 1911 to 4,000 in 1958. They virtually disappeared from the land in the 1960s, having given many centuries of strong and patient service. As the growing of cereals and sugar beet was profitably extended, the population of grazing animals declined. Between 1959 and 1981, the number of dairy cows in Suffolk fell by over 40 per cent and sheep by 55 per cent. By contrast, other animals multiplied

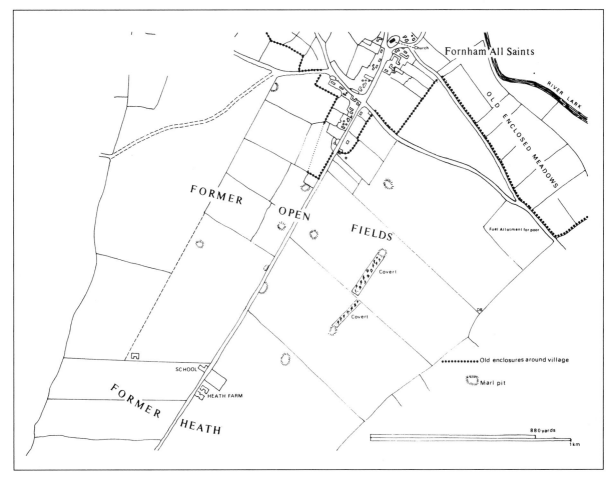

158 (left and above) *Landscapes of high Suffolk and Breckland in 1950: a manuscript map reveals that most hedges at Badingham already existed in 1614, although others were planted later to subdivide existing fields, and that the area then was mainly pasture and woodland; now arable with most of the ancient features destroyed. At Fornham, a geometric landscape of large fields, straight lines and marl-pits was created by Parliamentary enclosure in 1804 and, ironically, has survived much better than that at Badingham.*

159 *Offton: an example of the bleak empty landscapes caused in recent years by some arable farmers. Others, more sensitively, make major changes but still retain a sense of enclosure and continuity.*

160 *Snake's Head Fritillary, once common in Suffolk's meadows, still conserved in a few places.*

because they were intensively reared in special buildings. In the same period, pigs increased by 159 per cent to 617,200, more than in any other English county.

East Anglian fields of the 19th century normally yielded about 16 cwt of wheat per acre. In 1948 the barrier of 20 cwt was broken, and in 1962 that of 30 cwt; by 1984, yields had climbed to 60.6 cwt. This unprecedented improvement can be attributed to new strains of wheat, the chemical control of weeds and pests, and to the vastly increased use of chemical fertilisers.

The most dramatic human consequence of the farming revolution has been the dwindling number of agricultural workers. In 1901, Suffolk had 27,319 farm workers out of a total male workforce of 114,401 (24 per cent). By 1981, farms employed only 4,780 out of a total male workforce of 159,720 (3 per cent). The farming community as a whole accounted for only 5.3 per cent of the male working population, or 3.7 per cent of the total working population including women. While the industry has prospered economically, it has shrunk massively in terms of manpower. For the first time in their history, villages are no longer agricultural communities because the majority of their inhabitants do not depend on the land. Earlier this century, the social history of villages centred on the uneasy relationship between farmers and agricultural labourers. Now farmers find themselves increasingly out-numbered in a new rural society, largely middle-class and increasingly articulate, which is prepared to question their methods and to challenge their political influence.

The environmental results of the new Agricultural Revolution are huge and still incalculable. In about 40 years, the drive to mechanise farming and extend arable acreages has changed the Suffolk landscape faster and more radically than at any other time in its history. Using the modern technology of bulldozers, JCBs and power-saws, farmers and landowners have dismantled large parts of the traditional landscape which their predecessors created slowly by hand over many centuries. In most parishes, 50 per cent of the landscape features recorded on 19th-century maps have been destroyed (in some places, 70 per cent). They include hedges, ditches, road verges, green lanes, ponds, moats, woods and parish boundaries. All this happened without planning consent or public consultation, yet with the massive support of the taxpayer. Not surprisingly, this transformation has provoked much criticism and led to the development of an increasingly vocal conservationist lobby.

161 *Benjamin Britten (1913-76), composer and founder of Aldeburgh Festival.*

Yet the Suffolk landscape still contains a diversity which overall statistics conceal. On one side of a ditch, a particular farmer may have created a scene which is desolate, depressing and ecologically impoverished. On the other side, his neighbour may have found a successful compromise between modern efficiency and environmental responsibility: he may have removed many hedges and trees, but still retained a sense of enclosure and that vital thread of continuity from the past.

Religious life

In all probability, the churches in the early years of this century had more worshippers than at any other period of history. Furthermore, in 1914 for the first time since the Anglo-Saxon period, Suffolk achieved the distinction of its own bishopric. To reflect the ancient division of Suffolk, the new Anglican bishop was given the title of St Edmundsbury and Ipswich, having his cathedral in the former parish church of St James in Bury, and his residence in Ipswich.

In the 1980s, increasing numbers of abandoned chapels and redundant churches clearly indicate a decline in the appeal and status of organised religion. However, this decline is not easy to measure. The record of communicants does not fully reflect the strength of congregations, so perhaps the best evidence lies in the number of clergy and livings. In 1961 Suffolk had 540 clergy and ministers of religion (Anglican, nonconformist and Roman Catholic) but by 1981 the number had fallen to 280. Out of 516 Anglican benefices recorded in 1835, only 207 survived to 1983. In some cases, as many as eight parishes are now grouped together. Another measure may be found in the published membership of individual Anglican churches. Taking the Deanery of Hoxne as a sample, the 'electoral rolls' of its 20 constituent parishes fell from 2,006 in 1939 to 781 in 1983, yet those same 20 churches have the seating to accommodate 5,525 worshippers. In the same area, out of 13

162 *Bildeston church: dramatic collapse of the tower in 1975, caused by deterioration of the original lime mortar.*

163 *Badingham: unpretentious Primitive Methodist chapel built in 1836 at the eastern end of the parish.*

nonconformist chapels which existed in 1912, seven survived in 1983—including four which were Strict Baptist. In 1989 the only religious census to be attempted since 1851 found that 12 per cent of the adult population of Suffolk attended some form of worship.

The writings of clergy in this century have frequently complained of falling attendances and a declining interest in religion. The Rev. Arthur Ashton of Uggeshall and Sotherton wrote in 1936 of 'coldness and indifference' among a generation devoted to amusements such as the cinema, motorbikes and cars. Like many other clergy with shrinking incomes, he found the rectory too large and the gardens too costly to maintain.

The churches have undoubtedly lost touch with the majority of the population, and no longer have the social cachet which they once possessed, but this may have given them greater cohesion and strength. At the very least, they will remain important and influential minorities or pressure-groups in an increasingly diverse society. A recent development is the creation of non-denominational 'house-churches' of an evangelical or charismatic kind; these may yet prove to be historically significant.

Epilogue

164 *Tide Mill, Woodbridge: built in 1793 on a medieval site. Restoration completed 1976.*

The Suffolk of the 1990s is very different from that of 1900. It is no longer a depressed agricultural backwater, with an impoverished and demoralised population exporting its youth and much of its talent. Its agriculture has become efficient and prosperous (but now faces a far less certain future as a result of over-production) while the majority of its inhabitants work in commerce, manufacturing and service industries. A huge increase of population has been accommodated, and the standard of living has improved dramatically. Yet the best evidence that Suffolk is back in the forefront of national life lies in the problems and dangers which it faces. How do we plan economic growth without destroying local identity; reconcile mechanised, chemical farming with a countryside which is ancient, beautiful and fragile; house a rising population while still preserving a priceless heritage of historic towns and villages; plan future supplies of energy with safety for human beings and the environment? How do we combat the apathy and cynicism which devalues local democracy; and build a new regional consciousness which involves young and old, native and newcomer?

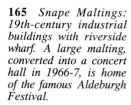

165 *Snape Maltings: 19th-century industrial buildings with riverside wharf. A large malting, converted into a concert hall in 1966-7, is home of the famous Aldeburgh Festival.*

Select Bibliography

Abbreviations: *VCH*: Victoria History of Suffolk; *PSIA*: Proceedings of the Suffolk Institute of Archaeology.

General Works
Alderton, D. and Booker, J., *The Batsford Guide to the Industrial Archaeology of East Anglia*, 1980; Blatchly, J., *The Topographers of Suffolk, 1561-1935*, 1988; Copinger, W.A., *Suffolk Records and Manuscripts*, 6 vols., 1904-07; Dymond, D. and Martin, E., eds., *An Historical Atlas of Suffolk*, 1989; Fincham, P., *The Suffolk We Live In*, 1976; Goult, W., ed., *A Survey of Suffolk Parish History*, 3 vols., 1990; Page, W., ed., *VCH*, 2 vols., 1907 and 1911; Pevsner, N., *The Buildings of England: Suffolk*, 1961, 1974; *PSIA*, 1848- ; Scarfe, N., *The Suffolk Landscape*, 1972; Scarfe, N., *The Suffolk Guide*, 1988; Steward, A.V., *A Suffolk Bibliography*, 1979.

1 Prehistory and the Romans
'The Barrows of East Anglia', *East Anglian Archaeology*, 12, 1981; Bland, R. and Johns, C., *The Hoxne Treasure*, 1993; Clarke, H., *East Anglia*, 1971; Clarke, R.R., *East Anglia*, 1960; Moore, I.E. *et al.*, *The Archaeology of Roman Suffolk*, 1988; Painter, K.S., *The Mildenhall Treasure*, 1977; Webster, G., *Boudica*, 1962, 1978; Wymer, J., *Palaeolithic sites of East Anglia*, 1985.

2 The Southfolk of the East Angles: *c*.400-1066
Bede, *A History of the English Church and People*, Penguin edn., 1955; Carver, M., *The Age of Sutton Hoo*, 1992; Evans, C.E., *The Sutton Hoo Ship Burial*, British Museum, 1986; Hart, C.R., *The Early Charters of Eastern England*, 1966; *PSIA*, Vol.XXI pt.3, 'Saint Edmund Commemorative Issue', 1970; Wade, K., *Origins of Ipswich*, 1981; West, S.E., *West Stow Anglo-Saxon Village*, 1985; Whitelock, D., ed., *The Anglo-Saxon Chronicle*, 1965; Whitelock, D., 'The pre-Viking Church in East Anglia', *Anglo-Saxon England*, I, 1972.

3 The Normans and English: 1066-1300
Butler, H.E., ed., *The Chronicle of Jocelin of Brakelond*, 1949; Darby, H.C., *The Domesday Geography of Eastern England*, 1952, 1957, 1971; Morris, J., ed., *Domesday Book: Suffolk*, 2 vols., Phillimore, 1986; Knowles, D. and Hadcock, R.N., *Medieval Religious Houses (England and Wales)*, 2nd edn., 1971; Page, W., ed., *VCH*, chapters on 'Ecclesiastical History' and 'Religious Houses', Vol.2, 1907; Powell, E., *A Suffolk Hundred in 1283*, 1910; Scarfe, N.,

166 *Ufford: 15th-century font-cover, 18 feet high.*

Suffolk in the Middles Ages, 1986; Smith, R.M., *The Sir Nicholas Bacon Collection*, Exhibition catalogue, 1972.

4 Crisis and Rebirth: 1300-1530

Betterton, A. and Dymond, D., *Lavenham: Industrial Town*, 1989; Dobson, R.B., ed., *The Peasants' Revolt of 1381*, 1970; Hervey, S.H.A., *Suffolk in 1327*, 1906; Hervey, S.H.A., *Suffolk in 1524*, 1910; Lobel, M.D., *Borough of Bury St Edmunds*, 1935; Page, W., ed., *VCH*, chapter on 'Industries', Vol.2, 1907; Pound, J., ed., *The Military Survey of 1522 for Babergh Hundred*, 1986; Suffolk Historic Churches Trust, *Suffolk Churches: a Pocket Guide*, 1976; Tanner, N.P., *Heresy Trials in the Diocese of Norwich 1428-31*, 1977; Ziegler, P., *The Black Death*, 1969.

5 Reformation and Division: 1530-1630

Collinson, P., *The Elizabethan Puritan Movement*, 1967; Duffy, E., *The Stripping of the Altars*, 1992; Dymond, D. and Paine, C., eds., *The Spoil of Melford Church*, 1992; Hervey, F., *Suffolk in the 17th Century: the Breviary of Suffolk by Robert Reyce*, 1902; MacCulloch, D., *The Chorography of Suffolk*, 1976; MacCulloch, D., *Suffolk and the Tudors*, 1986; Northeast, P., *Boxford Churchwardens' Accounts 1530-61*, 1982; Page, W., ed., *VCH*, chapter on 'Ecclesiastical History', Vol.2, 1907; Stow, T.Q., *Memories of Rowland Taylor ... an Account of the Rise of the Reformation in the Counties of Norfolk and Suffolk*, 1833; Thirsk, J., ed., *The Agrarian History of England and Wales, Vol.IV 1500-1640*, 1967.

6 War and Turmoil: 1630-1710

Blome, J., *Britannia*, 1673; Browne, J., *History of Congregationalism in Norfolk and Suffolk*, 1877; Defoe, D., *Tour through the Eastern Counties*, 1949; Everitt, A., *Suffolk and the Great Rebellion 1640-60*, 1960; Halliwell, J.O., ed., *Autobiography and Correspondence of Sir Simonds D'Ewes*, 2 vols., 1845; Hervey, S.H.A., *Suffolk in 1674*, 1905; Holmes, C., *The Suffolk Committees for Scandalous Ministers 1644-46*, 1970; Kingston, A., *East Anglia and the Great Civil War*, 1897; Page, W., ed., *VCH*, chapter on 'Maritime History', Vol.2, 1907; Thirsk, J., ed., *The Agrarian History of England and Wales, Vol.V, 1640-1750*, 1985.

7 Georgian Suffolk: 1710-1800

Anon., *Description of England and Wales*, Vols.8 and 9 for Suffolk, 1769; Dymond D.P., ed., *The County of Suffolk Surveyed by Joseph Hodskinson, 1783*, 1972; Evans, N., *The East Anglian Linen Industry: Rural Industry and Local Economy, 1500-1850*, 1985; Hervey, S.H.A., *The Diary of John Hervey, 1st Earl of Bristol*, 1894; Kenworthy-Browne, J., *Burke's and Savills Guide to Country Houses, Vol.III: East Anglia*, 1981; Kirby, J., *The Suffolk Traveller*, 1735 and 1764; Scarfe, N., ed., *A Frenchman's Year in Suffolk, 1784*, 1988; *Suffolk Review*, Vol.5, No.1, 'Popular Disturbances in Suffolk', 1980; Young, A., *General View of the Agriculture of the County of Suffolk*, 1797 and 1813.

8 An Agricultural County in an Industrial Age: 1800-1900

Archer, J., *By a Flash and a Scare*, 1990; Clifford, F., *The Agricultural Lock-out of 1874*, 1875; Crabbe, G., *The Borough*, 1810; *Directories* (commercial) from 1839 onwards, by various publishers—Robson, Kelly, White, Harrod, etc.; Glyde, J., *Suffolk in the 19th Century*, c.1856; Shoberl, F., *The Beauties of England and Wales: Suffolk*, 1812-13; *Suffolk Review*, Vol.5, No.2, 'Aspects of Education', 1981, and Vol.5, No.4, 'Some Suffolk Industries', 1983; Thirsk, J. and Imray, J., *Suffolk Farming in the Nineteenth Century*, 1958.

9 Stagnation and Revival: 1900-85

Blythe, R., *Akenfield*, 1969; Evans, G.E., *Ask the Fellows who cut the Hay*, 1956; Francis, L.J., *Rural Anglicanism*, 1985 (the unnamed diocese in this survey is St Edmundsbury and Ipswich); Goffin, J.R., ed., *The Carlton Colville Chronicles of Canon Reginald Augustus Bignold*, 1982; Haggard, H.R., *Rural England*, Vol.2, 1902; Harrison, C., *Victorian and Edwardian Suffolk from old Photographs*, 1973; Jennings, C., *The Identity of Suffolk*, 1980; Jennings, C., ed., *Suffolk for Ever*, 1989; Oxenbury, T.B., and Abercromby, P., *Suffolk Planning Survey*, 1946; Tennyson, J., *Suffolk Scene*, 1939; Trist, P.J.O., *A Survey of the Agriculture of Suffolk*, 1971.

Index

Note: figures in **bold** refer to illustration numbers.